MICHAEL JORDAN

BEYOND THE COURT

By The Associated Press

Mango Media
Miami
in collaboration with
The Associated Press

AP   AP EDITIONS

AP Editions

Copyright © 2015 Associated Press. All rights reserved. This material may not be published, broadcast, rewritten or redistributed.

Published by Mango Media, Inc.
www.mangomedia.us

No part of this publication may be reproduced, distributed or transmitted in any form or by any means, without prior written permission.

This is a work of non-fiction adapted from articles and content by journalists of The Associated Press and published with permission.

Michael Jordan *Beyond the Court*
ISBN: 978-1-63353-149-9

Cover Photo:

Chicago Bulls' Michael Jordan takes part in the NBA All-Star Slam Dunk contest in Seattle, Washington, February 7, 1987. (AP Photo/Kirthmon Dozier)

Publisher's Note

AP Editions brings together stories and photographs by the professional journalists of The Associated Press.

These stories are presented in their original form and are intended to provide a snapshot of history as the moments occurred.

We hope you enjoy these selections from the front lines of newsgathering.

"Everything's been painted as a golden stream to a championship, but dealing with expectations is sometimes hard. It's dangerous, because you can fall prey to that and forget about playing the game and doing your job."

Michael Jordan, June 11, 1996

Table of Contents

Overview 1
North Carolina Tar Heels 3
3rd Overall Pick 17
The Dream Team Legacy 51
Drugs, Gambling, Death and Baseball 67
Three More Rings 97
One Last Run 129
Turmoil in Washington 147
Businessman 161
Billionaire Owner 171
Greatest Ever 179
Afterword 183

Overview

Michael Jordan may be the greatest professional athlete of our time. He is an NCAA basketball champion, a two-time Olympic gold medalist, a six-time NBA champion, and the face of Nike.

You know him as "Air Jordan." Or "His Airness." Or maybe you wanted to "Be Like Mike."

During his career, Jordan changed how basketball is viewed around the world and showed how marketing and sports culture can transform a player from a mainstream athlete into a global icon.

Here are the moments where Jordan captivated the world as he transcended beyond the court. With the stunning sports photography and reporting of The Associated Press, experience the exceptional career of Michael Jordan.

North Carolina Tar Heels

Past on Display
March 31, 1995
By Estes Thompson

North Carolina guard Michael Jordan (23) goes up as University of Arkansas guard Alvin Robertson tries to block during the game in Pine Bluff, Arkansas, February 12, 1984. (AP Photo/Jeff Bowen)

Now, Michael Jordan is a part of the natural history of southeastern North Carolina.

Jordan's image, voice and items from his high school and college days are the hook to attract children to the Michael Jordan Discovery Gallery at the

Cape Fear Museum. Once in, the children will be educated about the region and perhaps be inspired by Jordan.

"We want to reach kids and let them know that it did not all start with basketball for Michael," his mother, Deloris Jordan, said as she toured the 1,200-square-foot gallery, still under construction. "It is the values he learned at home that instilled the desire to do his best."

Mrs. Jordan will be with her famous son for a private sponsors' party the day before the June 25 public opening.

Major funding was provided by Jordan's family, not his charitable foundation. The local Junior League gave $18,000 and hours of volunteer time.

The gallery will cost about $200,000, a modest sum in museum terms, said Harry Warren, assistant director at the museum. The amount of the Jordans' contribution, acknowledged as the largest, is confidential.

"The Jordan family has built this to contribute back to the community," Mrs. Jordan said. "No matter where we go, this will always be home. No matter how much somebody else wants to claim us, they can't."

The natural history exhibit will have things like the Talking Tree, Nature's Teabag, a model beaver lodge children can crawl into, and a huge venus flytrap model fed with beanbags tossed by visitors.

As interesting as those items may be, it's Jordan's possessions from his youth that make the museum a must on any fan's pilgrimage.

The items will be displayed in a 10-foot glass case outside the gallery. Jordan will star in a video about growing up in Wilmington.

There's the pine box he made in shop class and took to the University of North Carolina-Chapel Hill. The box has "Feb. 17 ... Mike Jordan ... Aquarius" etched on the lid and bears the residue of adhesive tape used to keep it closed.

There's the collection of gym bags and uniforms; a picture of Jordan in a football uniform; his baseball cap from a Dixie Youth Baseball tournament in 1982. Mrs. Jordan crooned as she and museum director Janet Seapker dug through boxes of items: a Carolina blue, fuzzy Christmas stocking; more caps; towels; warm-up suits; his UNC graduation gown; trophies.

University of Houston's Clyde Drexler, center, grabs the rebound as University of North Carolina players Michael Jordan (23) and Matt Doherty (44) get in the action during NCAA semi-final play in New Orleans, March 28, 1982. North Carolina won. (AP Photo)

Houston's Clyde Drexler, left, and North Carolina's Michael Jordan, 23, battle for the ball, during NCAA semifinal final game played at the Superdome in New Orleans, March 29, 1982. (AP Photo)

There are letters from Dean Smith's office trying to lure Jordan. In one, Smith thanks Mrs. Jordan for making him a meal on one visit. There's the letter of intent Jordan signed for UNC on March 17, 1981. There's a cake recipe from a home economics class.

In a college term paper on Jordan's USA team winning the 1984 Olympics he writes: "My eyes were misting from almost tears but my heart was so happy I could feel and hear it beating loudly.

"Many a game is won or lost because of mental errors," he wrote.

There's Jordan's boating safety certificate and a middle school certificate for good humor, "for being able to make jokes, take jokes and for being able to laugh at one's self."

The items had been stored in Mrs. Jordan's home near Charlotte. Now, they get museum care. Tim Bottoms, registrar of artifacts, donned white gloves to catalog them.

The museum staff is excited about the gallery's potential. Since Jordan abandoned pro baseball and returned to the Chicago Bulls, they follow the basketball games and whooped it up when Jordan scored 55 points against the Knicks.

Wilmington already is comfortable with Jordan's fame. People still seek out the house where he grew up on Gordon Road, and a section of Interstate 40 entering town is named in his honor.

1982 Still Resonates Today
March 28, 2002
By Aaron Beard

Mike Jordan waited on the left wing. With his team down by one and a national championship at stake, the skinny, 19-year-old freshman was virtually unnoticed by the defense as the final seconds ticked away.

One jump shot made sure that would never happen again.

Jordan has made nearly 30 game-winning shots in his pro career, including one that gave the Chicago Bulls their sixth NBA championship. But none was bigger than the one he hit 20 years ago Friday: a 16-foot jumper with 15 seconds left to give North Carolina the 1982 NCAA championship.

And it introduced Michael Jordan to the world.

"That's THE shot," Jordan said. "That's the one that initiated everything. If I put anything ahead of that, honestly, I wouldn't be who I am."

North Carolina and Georgetown met in New Orleans for the NCAA championship on March 29, 1982. Trailing 62-61 with the ball in the final seconds, the Tar Heels called timeout.

Coach Dean Smith wanted to get the ball inside to James Worthy _ who finished with a game-high 28 points _ or Sam Perkins. The 6-foot-5, 188-pound Jordan _ listed as "Mike" in the Tar Heels media guide _ was the third option.

"As he was walking out of the huddle, I told him, 'If it comes to you, knock it in,'" Smith said.

Sophomore forward Matt Doherty swung the ball rightside to point guard Jimmy Black, who dribbled back toward the top of the key and lofted a pass over the defense to Jordan.

Jordan didn't hesitate, releasing the ball as the Georgetown defense rotated toward him. With 15 seconds to play, the shot swished through.

The final score was 63-62. It was Smith's first national championship.

"As I look at that shot, even to this day, I'm just amazed that a freshman had the poise and confidence to take that shot in that situation," said Doherty, now North Carolina's coach.

"The thing to make note of is that he didn't have to shoot the ball," Doherty said. "It wasn't like there was just one or two seconds on the clock. And it wasn't like he was wide, wide open. He could've pump-faked and kicked it out.

"But he wanted to take that shot. He shot it like he was in a shooting drill. He put the ball up and it went right through heart of the rim."

There seemed to be little doubt on the Tar Heels' bench. Photos of the moment show Smith and his assistant coaches _ Bill Guthridge, Roy Williams and Eddie Fogler _ in the background, sitting on the bench with calm expressions.

"It sure looked good when it left his hand," Smith said.

Jordan said the shot gave him added confidence. Doherty said it was more: No. 23 developed an aura.

"There was a presence about him," Doherty said.

Michael Jordan

Georgetown's Ed Springs grabs a rebound ahead of North Carolina's Michael Jordan (23) during the NCAA championship game in New Orleans. Jordan scored 16 points including the winning basket as North Carolina won the game, 63-62, March 30, 1982. (AP Photo)

North Carolina's Michael Jordan (23) cheers from the bench as the Tar Heels wins another game for head coach Dean Smith, right, in Raleigh, North Carolina, November 15 1983. (AP Photo/Bob Jordan)

Early the next season, Jordan stole an inbounds pass and hit a long jumper at the buzzer to tie a game against Tulane. North Carolina would go on to take a 70-68 triple-overtime win, avoiding an 0-3 start.

Later that year, Jordan had a steal and breakaway dunk in the final minute that completed a 16-point rally to beat Ralph Sampson and Virginia 64-63.

Other last-minute Jordan highlights:

- During an exhibition tour in Greece before the 1983-84 season, the Tar Heels trailed Red Star of Yugoslavia by one in the final seconds. Perkins deflected a pass, Jordan recovered and drained a 7-footer to give North Carolina a 105-104 double-overtime win.

- Once Jordan suited up for the Bulls, he made the dramatic shot so often that it became almost routine. Most remember the hanging jumper at the foul line over Craig Ehlo to eliminate the

Cleveland Cavaliers from the 1989 playoffs. Even more recognizable was his final shot with the Bulls _ a championship-clinching jumper over Utah's Byron Russell in Game 6 of the 1998 NBA Finals.

Jordan, now with the Washington Wizards, said it all started two decades ago in the Superdome.

"It was a stage that I stepped on," Jordan remembered. "From that point on, I felt like I was obligated to become the best basketball player I could become."

Coach Dean Smith
January 14, 1999
By Chris Duncan

The greatest player in the history of North Carolina basketball almost didn't play for the Tar Heels.

Former UNC coach Dean Smith reminisced about recruiting Michael Jordan hours after the NBA superstar announced his retirement in Chicago on Wednesday.

"He really liked UCLA, but I guess they didn't call him," said Smith, who remains one of Jordan's closest friends. "He wasn't the most highly recruited kid at that time, but we were delighted to have him.

"We recognized his determination, and we recognized he had great quickness and speed, but we had no idea about his basketball savvy."

Jordan went on to star for North Carolina, hitting the title-clinching shot as a freshman in the 1982 NCAA championship game. He left Chapel Hill after his junior season and was drafted by the Chicago Bulls in 1984.

The rest is history, and Smith, who retired in 1997 as college basketball's winningest coach, said Wednesday he was astonished by Jordan's list of achievements.

"He was the national player of the year in 1984, but we never dreamed here, 14 or 15 years later, he would accomplish what he's accomplished," said Smith, who remains one of Jordan's closest friends. "I think it's remarkable that every year he improved. He really is special.

"I'm happy for him now. At this point, he's happy, his teams have won and what more could you want from anyone you care about?"

Smith said he wouldn't be surprised if Jordan returned to the sports spotlight in another form.

"If he attempts to be a senior golfer at 50, do not be surprised if he is successful," Smith said. "He really got a bad rap when he tried baseball. More and more baseball people told me he could've done it. It was going to take time, but he was improving."

Former North Carolina basketball coach Dean Smith smiles as he signs a copy of his autobiography "A Coach's Life: My Forty Years in College Basketball" at the Bull's Head Bookshop in Chapel Hill. North Carolina, November 8, 1999. (AP Photo/Grant Halverson)

Former North Carolina player Michael Jordan, left, gives his former coach Dean Smith a kiss during halftime of a college basketball game between North Carolina and Wake Forest. The 1982 and 1957 championship teams were recognized during a halftime ceremony. Jordan was a member of the 1982 team in Chapel Hill, North Carolina, February 10, 2007. (AP Photo/Gerry Broome)

Jimmy Black, who assisted on Jordan's NCAA title-winning shot in 1982, said he had thought that James Worthy, another member of that team, had a better shot at basketball superstardom than Jordan.

"You could tell (Jordan) would be good because of how hard he was willing to work, but no one could have imagined all this," Black told The News & Observer of Raleigh.

Matt Doherty, another member of the 1982 championship team and now an assistant coach at Kansas, said he knew in May that Jordan would retire.

"When I heard he wasn't working in the offseason, it only confirmed things because Michael would never go into a season unprepared," Doherty said.

"He entertained us for many years and for that we should all thank him. The game will sorely miss him."

Smith said Jordan's most remarkable characteristic is the way he handled what has become worldwide media scrutiny.

"I have so many great memories of him, I couldn't begin to start with one," Smith said. "I'm still amazed at how he handled something that's impossible to do _ the adoration. It's amazing how he survives with so much attention given to him.

"He hit a clutch putt for me once. I'll remember that, too."

Mentor, Teacher...2nd Father
February 8, 2015
By Steve Reed

North Carolina guard Michael Jordan, left, and Tar Heels coach Dean Smith are shown at a news conference in Chapel Hill, N.C., where Jordan announced he would forfeit his final year of college eligibility to turn pro, May 5, 1984. (AP Photo, File)

Michael Jordan called North Carolina coaching great Dean Smith the most influential person in his life other than his parents.

Smith died Saturday night, February 7, 2015, at 83.

In a statement on Twitter released through his business manager, Jordan said Smith was "more than a coach — he was a mentor, my teacher, my second father."

The former NBA superstar and Charlotte Hornets owner said "In teaching me the game of basketball, he taught me about life."

Jordan played three seasons for Smith from 1981-84. When he was a freshman he helped lead the Tar Heels to a national championship in 1982, hitting a 16-foot jump shot in the final seconds to beat Georgetown.

Jordan often said that shot was the turning point in his basketball career. He went on to win six titles and is considered by many the greatest basketball player ever.

Through the years, Jordan's respect for Smith grew, and he would often lean on his beloved college coach for advice and guidance.

"Coach was always there for me whenever I needed him and I loved him for it," Jordan said in the statement.

Former Chicago Bulls great Michael Jordan shares a moment with Dean Smith, his former coach at North Carolina, during ceremonies honoring Jordan at Chicago's United Center, November 1, 1994. (AP Photo/Pool, File)

At Jordan's Hall of Fame acceptance speech, he called Smith "legendary." Jordan also poked some fun at him — as he often did — about his days as a freshman and a Sports Illustrated cover.

"The day that he was on the Sports Illustrated and he named four starters and he didn't name me — that burned me up," Jordan joked in the speech. "Because I thought I belonged on that Sports Illustrated. Now he had his own vision about giving a freshman that exposure, and I totally understand that. But from a basketball sense I deserved to be on that Sports Illustrated."

In 2007, Jordan returned to Chapel Hill for a game honoring the Tar Heels championship team in 1982. He was photographed with his arm around Smith and kissing the gray-haired coach on his head.

"My heart goes out to Linnea and their kids," Jordan said. "We've lost a great man who had an incredible impact on his players his staff and the entire UNC family."

Charlotte Bobcats owner Michael Jordan, left, stands with former North Carolina coach Dean Smith, right, as they watch a video presentation at halftime of an NBA basketball game between the Charlotte Bobcats and the Toronto Raptors in Charlotte, North Carolina, December 14, 2010. (AP Photo)

3rd Overall Pick

Reflecting on the Rookie of the Year
April 8, 1997
By Mike Nadel

NBA All Stars Allen Iverson, left, of the Philadelphia 76ers, Jason Kidd, second from left, of the New Jersey Nets, Ray Allen, third from left, of the Milwaukee Bucks, and Michael Jordan, right, of the Washington Wizards, joke around during the Eastern Conference All Star practice in Philadelphia, February 9, 2002. (AP Photo/Chris Gardner)

It's fashionable to tout Minnesota's Stephon Marbury, Vancouver's Shareef Abdur-Rahim and Boston's Antoine Walker for NBA Rookie of the Year honors.

Philadelphia's Allen Iverson? He's a punk. A trash-talker. A ball hog. A brash kid who even dissed Michael Jordan early this season.

He's also the best choice for top rookie. At least, that's what Jordan thinks. "Because of the excitement that he brings," the Chicago star said, "he's the leading candidate without a doubt."

Jordan even compared Iverson to himself Monday night in the closing minutes of the Bulls' 128-102 victory over the 76ers.

After Iverson sliced through four Bulls to score two of his career-high 44 points, Jordan turned to press row and said: "Was I a one-man offense like that when I was a rookie? I just wanted to know because it was so long ago."

Jordan, the NBA's all-time leader in scoring average and the 1985 Rookie of the Year, later said he could play alongside Iverson even though each likes to look for his own shot first.

"If he's hot, I have to feed it to him," Jordan said. "If we win, great. If we're losing, we're going to have to compete for those shots."

It's interesting that Jordan has so many nice things to say about Iverson because the rookie's image took a tumble early this season after the two got into a disagreement on the court. Among other things, Iverson said he didn't have to respect Jordan, perhaps the best player ever to lace up sneakers.

Chicago Bulls' guard, Michael Jordan in uniform in 1984. (AP Photo)

"I feel like I deserve it, and I want the award," Iverson said. "But ever since that incident, the media has been on me. It's like, `He said something to Michael Jordan, so let's dog him.' If something like that can cost me the award, then the award is not worth getting."

Many voting members of the media have said they were leaning toward Marbury, who has helped turn Minnesota from perennial doormat into a contender. Others like Abdur-Rahim or Walker.

But Iverson's 22-point average leads all first-year players by far. And he has had to perform under an intense spotlight because of his perceived cockiness.

Even NBA bad boys like Charles Barkley and Dennis Rodman have taken shots at Iverson, who has been called the poster child for everything that's wrong with today's young players.

"I don't care what somebody says about me off the court," Iverson said.

"Those guys don't know me. They just judge me from what is in the paper and what they hear on the street. I think it's unfair, but that's life."

Iverson, like Jordan years ago, has been accused of being a selfish gunner. He took 32 shots Monday, making 16. But he also had eight assists.

"At Georgetown, I was used to scoring. Whenever my team needed a basket, they went to me," he said. "Now, we've got guys like Derrick Coleman, Clarence Weatherspoon and Jerry Stackhouse. I'll keep trying to get assists, but I always look for my baskets. That's what got me into the NBA."

20 AP Editions

Chicago Bulls' Michael Jordan, left, receives NBA's Rookie of the Year trophy from an unidentified NBA official during NBA's award ceremony in San Francisco, June 24, 1985. (AP Photo/Paul Sakuma)

Chicago Bulls' Michael Jordan (23) guards Philadelphia 76ers Allen Iverson (3) during an exhibition game at the Dean Smith Center, in Chapel Hill, North Carolina, October 24, 1997. (AP Photo/ Karl DeBlaker)

Washington Wizards' Michael Jordan (23) tries to get past Philadelphia 76ers' Allen Iverson, left, during second half action of the 76ers' 88-80 win, January 18, 2003. (AP Photo/Nick Wass)

Michael Jordan 23

All-Star Weekend
February 7, 1988

Michael Jordan of the Chicago Bulls dunks during the slam-dunk competition of the NBA All-Star weekend in Chicago, Illinois, February 6, 1988. (AP Photo/John Swart)

Chicago Bulls' Michael Jordan dunks the ball during the Slam-Dunk championship in Chicago as a part of the NBA All-Star weekend. Jordan edged Atlanta Hawks' Dominique Wilkins on the final dunk to win the contest, February, 6, 1988. (AP Photo/John Swart)

Michael Jordan holds the trophy for Most Valuable Player after the NBA All-Star game in Chicago He was the unanimous choice for the title, February 7, 1988. (AP Photo/Fred Jewell)

New Heights
May 14, 1988
By Bill Barnard

Chicago Bulls' Michael Jordan (23) drives for the basket past Cleveland Cavaliers' defender Craig Ehlo during the fourth quarter of the NBA playoff in Richfield Coliseum, Ohio, May 4, 1988. Cleveland won 110-102. (AP Photo/Mark Duncan)

Michael Jordan's been called a monster, Superman and God by opponents in the NBA.

Jordan's mother, Deloris, knows better.

"He shocks me with some of the things he does out there on the court, but I know he's human," Mrs. Jordan said. "I was there when he was born."

Before Tuesday's opener of the Eastern Conference semifinal playoffs between Jordan's Chicago Bulls and the Detroit Pistons, Jordan was casually lacing up a new pair of Air Jordans when a young boy, part of the halftime tumbling show, shyly stepped forward.

"Can I look at your shoes?" he asked, then inspected them with wondrous eyes, searching for the secret within. Handing them back, the youngster said, "These will be flyin' later on."

Two hours later, those shoes indeed were flying on Jordan's feet, but not as high as he had become accustomed in the playoffs.

In the opener against the Pistons, he was 10-for-22 from the field and scored 29 points.

"We did everything possible and he still ended up with 29," Pistons coach Chuck Daly said."He's a monster."

Larry Bird sees it differently.

"It's just God disguised as Michael Jordan," the Boston star said in April, 1986, after Jordan came back from a broken foot to score 131 pointed in three playoff games against the Celtics, including 63 in one game.

Jordan, who averaged 35.0 points and shot 53 percent from the field during this regular season, upped the ante to 45.2 points and 56 percent shooting in his first five playoff games, all against Cleveland.

"Guarding him is an honor, a thrill, a challenge, a nightmare," the Cavaliers' Craig Ehlo said. "It's all instincts with him. He has no tendencies. Everything's spontaneous; he just does it."

But as Jordan soared to 226 points, an NBA playoff record for a five-game series, questions resurfaced about whether a scoring champion can ever lead a team to a championship.

"If I didn't believe it, I wouldn't want to play," Jordan said. "The team is better this season. I'm getting better shots this season because I'm not having to force it."

Bulls coach Doug Collins said the balance issue is overblown because it puts too much stress on scoring.

"In the first two games against Cleveland, he carried us with 55 and 50 points," Collins said. "But in Game 5, everybody contributed. It's not always points that determine how you're playing. There's so much focus on Jordan's scoring, people forget that we led the league in defense and rebounding."

Whether the Bulls can win a title with Jordan scoring 44.3 percent of the team's points, as he did against Cleveland, or even 33.3 percent, as he did in the regular season, remains to be seen.

"Two years ago, this team won 30 games, so I'm proud that people even mention us as a championship threat," Collins said. "So I'm not worrying about having enough scoring balance."

"There are nights that I'm going to produce big offensively, and there are nights when the other guys are going to do more," Jordan said. "That's true whether you're talking about the regular season or the playoffs. When Scottie Pippen scored 24 points against Cleveland, for the first time people were not talking about me so much."

Jordan said he expects more physical defense against him during the playoffs, especially the hard-nosed Pistons.

"Cleveland bumped me a lot more, and I expected that," Jordan said. "I had to prepare myself mentally for this kind of intensity. These are games that can send you home if you lose.

"The Cavaliers were more physical than you see in a regular-season game against the Pistons. But now it's up another notch and the Pistons will be even more physical."

Isiah Thomas, Detroit's leading scorer in the playoffs, said Jordan gets away with a physical move to get free of a defense.

"He's as good as anybody in the league at throwing you away to get open," Thomas said. "When he's allowed to grab you and throw you away from him, that puts him three steps off the ball. If the officials can be conscious of him doing that, then we'll have a chance.

"But you can't guard him anyway. I want to make that clear. You can't guard him anyway."

"All you can do is put a hand in his face and hope he misses."

Thomas sympathizes with Jordan's plight of having to carry such a big offensive load with the Bulls. Before the arrival of Adrian Dantley, Joe Dumars, Dennis Rodman and John Salley, Thomas had a similar burden.

"It's a tough load to carry because you have to play 48 hard minutes, and every time you get the ball, all eyes are on you," Thomas said. "It's a heavy load to carry."

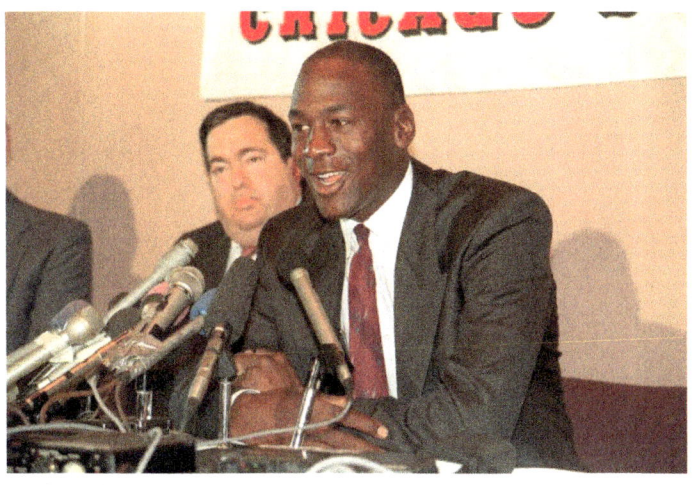

At left is Bulls General Manager Jerry Kraus. Michael Jordan of the Chicago Bulls speaks at a news conference after he signed an eight-year extension to his contract in Chicago, Ill., September 20, 1988. (AP Photo/Mark Elias)

Jordan admitted there is a danger that if he becomes too dominant, his teammates might simply watch him in awe.

"But it's only an offensive concern during the playoffs," Jordan said. "On defense, everyone has to be more intense. The intensity level is higher because the prize is more prestigious. Sure, the ball will come to me more when I'm on a roll, but I try to pick my spots offensively."

Thomas doesn't believe that beating Chicago is just a matter of slowing down Jordan.

"They're capable of beating us without a superhuman effort from Michael because the other guys are very good basketball players," Thomas said.

After all, Jordan's only human. Just ask his mom.

Chicago Bulls' Michael Jordan shoots off-balance with six seconds left in the game against the New York Knicks in Chicago, May 20, 1989. The Bulls won, 113-111. (AP Photo/John Swart)

Looking for Help
March 18, 1989
By Mario Fox

Chicago Bulls' Michael Jordan (23) stops dead in his tracks to block a shot by Cleveland Cavaliers' Mark Price (25) as Bulls' Horace Grant (54) watches during first period action, May 3, 1989. (AP Photo/Mark Elias)

Michael Jordan is truly the Superman of basketball, but his supporting cast on the Chicago Bulls might as well include Lois Lane or Jimmy Olsen.

"He's the greatest. He's from another planet," says Dick Versace, coach of the Indiana Pacers.

Could he be referring to the planet Krypton?

Actually, some fear Jordan's hard-nose style of play and the Bulls' dependence on him could be to him what Kryptonite was to the Man of Steel.

"If Michael has to do this year after year, it will shorten his career," says Atlanta star Dominique Wilkins.

Suddenly, Jordan has switched roles and become a point guard at least on a part-time basis, a move fans in Metropolis - er, Chicago - hope will bring the Bulls something they've never had - a measure of success in the NBA playoffs.

A year ago, Jordan won the NBA scoring title, and was named the league's Most Valuable Player, Defensive Player of the Year and All-Star MVP. This season, he leads the league in scoring again, with an average of 33 points a game.

The high-flying No. 23, known as Air Jordan for his acrobatic style of play, is the best all-around player currently in the NBA, according to Rich Share's Basketball Computer Ratings.

But, in four previous years with Jordan on the team, and even going back to when the franchise was founded in 1966, the Bulls have never won a second-round playoff series.

Through Thursday, the Bulls had a respectable winning percentage of .590, but they were in fifth place in the tough NBA Central Division, and still having trouble with teams they need to beat if they want to go far in the playoffs - Cleveland, New York, Philadelphia, Milwaukee and Detroit.

Jordan and his coach, Doug Collins, sat down recently to discuss what they could do to sharpen the Bulls' horns.

"We came to an agreement about things we must do in order to gain some ground on the teams in front of us," says Jordan.

One idea they came up with was moving Jordan from second guard - also known as scoring guard or off guard - to point or play-making guard.

Chicago Bulls Michael Jordan argues a baseline call with official Jess Kersey during action against the New York Knicks at New York's Madison Square Garden, May 16, 1989. The Knicks beat the Bulls 121-114. (AP Photo/Susan Ragan)

Jordan, 26, ran the offense for the first time on March 11 against Seattle and had 18 points, 15 assists and eight rebounds. Although Jordan tied his season low for scoring, Chicago beat the SuperSonics 105-88.

Next game he got 21 points, 14 rebounds and 14 assists, three steals and two blocked shots as Chicago beat Versace's Pacers 122-90, the team's biggest margin of victory all season. Jordan played a season-tying low 30 minutes against Indiana."I was able to rebound, start the fast break, pass off or score," Jordan explains.

Versace says the switch keeps Jordan from becoming worn out trying to score all the time and Collins says it keeps his star from being double and triple teamed.

But critics say the Bulls still must get better 'company' for Jordan & Co.

"Michael plays it down, but he's a one-man team," says Sam Perkins, a Dallas Maverick who played with Jordan at North Carolina.

With Jordan sidelined with a groin injury, the Bulls lost 104-95 on March 8 to a Boston team without Larry Bird. It was the first time in three years Jordan had missed a game.

"A lot of times they looked a little lost out there offensively. It was like they were looking for Michael," says Boston center Joe Kleine.

Chicago guard John Paxton thinks Jordan is so much better than his teammates, "It must be like most of the rest of us playing with grade school kids."

Milwaukee's Ricky Pierce doesn't believe Jordan will burn himself out soon.

"He's a great basketball player. He'll be able to play at his current pace for another five, six years," says Pierce.

In December, the Bulls acquired shooting guard Craig Hodges from Phoenix, but General Manager Jerry Krause warns that the team has been limited in finding quality players because Jordan's eight-year, $25 million contract puts the team near the NBA salary limit.

The team is still smarting from criticism for trading rebound leader Charles Oakley to the New York Knicks for center Bill Cartwright.

Jordan thinks Oakley's "tough image" is sorely missed.

Somebody else - perhaps forwards Scottie Pippen or Horace Grant? Or guard Sam Vincent? - apparently needs to step forward, play more aggressively and take some pressure off Jordan.

Terry Cummings of the Bucks doesn't think the Bulls need to do much more to become a factor in the NBA title race.

"It's actually more other people picking up, and Mike just being consistent with what he does," said Cummings.

The Bad Boy Pistons
December 24, 1996
By Mike Nadel

An NBA era ago, a young Michael Jordan kept trying to climb to the top of the basketball world, only to be slammed back to earth by the "Bad Boy" Detroit Pistons.

Now, Grant Hill is knocking, and Jordan's Chicago Bulls want to keep slamming the door in the young Detroit star's face.

"We're a measuring stick for the Pistons, as they were for us back in '88 and '89," said Jordan, whose Bulls play host to Detroit in a Christmas night matchup between the teams with the NBA's best records.

"Each time we saw them, we tried to see how much we had progressed. Now they're trying to get over the hump, and we want to keep them right where they are."

Second place is where the Pistons are. Detroit (20-5) trails the defending champion Bulls (24-3) by three games in the Central Division. They are the only two NBA teams with winning percentages of at least .800.

"They're playing well and are capable of having a great game, so we're going to be up for it," said Scottie Pippen, another survivor of the battles against Bad Boys Dennis Rodman, Bill Laimbeer and Rick Mahorn. "It's a compliment to be chosen to play on Christmas. It's special, and we're going to treat it that way."

The Pistons-Bulls game is the second half of a nationally televised doubleheader that also includes the Los Angeles Lakers at the Phoenix Suns.

"My parents are at home and I don't have any family in Detroit, so I'd rather spend Christmas with Michael and Scottie," said Hill, whose personable manner and wonderful talent have led many to dub him the next Jordan.

Chicago Bulls' Michael Jordan (23) sticks out his tongue as he shoots past Detroit Pistons' Joe Dumars (4) during game at night in Chicago, February 10, 1988. The Pistons beat the Bull 89-74. (AP Photo/Fred Jewell)

Chicago Bulls Michael Jordan (23) tries to block a shot from Detroit Pistons John Salley in game 4 of the Eastern Conference playoffs, Chicago, Ill, May 28, 1990. (AP Photo/Jim Mone)

The Bulls lost to the Pistons in the 1988, 1989 and 1990 playoffs. Detroit won NBA titles in '89 and '90. In 1991, the Bulls finally got past the Pistons and began their string of four championships in six years.

The Pistons are looking for a breakthrough game, having lost 17 consecutive times to the Bulls since last winning on March 14, 1993. That was so long ago that Rodman was on the Pistons; he's now in his second season with the Bulls after spending two years with the San Antonio Spurs.

After Chicago won 98-80 at Detroit on Nov. 8, Pistons coach Doug Collins said: "They are one of the greatest teams of all-time, maybe the greatest. No team in the NBA can play with them right now."

Collins, who coached the Bulls from 1986-89, hopes his team has closed the gap in the seven weeks since.

Chicago guard Steve Kerr said the Bulls respect the Pistons.

"We've handled them pretty easily lately, but we take them very seriously," Kerr said. "They play very hard and have great shooters. Grant Hill is incredible. They've been playing great defense, too."

It will be Jordan's first Christmas game since 1992. He didn't play in the following two seasons and, after coming out of retirement, his Bulls weren't chosen to play on the holiday last year.

"It brings back some memories," said Jordan, who is 3-1 on Christmas.

The Pistons hope to start some new fond memories of their own.

"Most people don't want to be playing on Christmas and don't want to be playing the Bulls," Hill said. "But I look forward to playing against the best team in the world with the whole world watching."

First Ring
June 13, 1991
By Stanley D. Miller

Partying fans packed downtown streets early today, hours after the Chicago Bulls won the first NBA championship in their 25-year history. Cheering fans erupted from the homes and taverns as the Bulls took the NBA Finals with a 108-101 victory over the Lakers in Los Angeles Wednesday night.

Traffic ground to a halt on several major city streets. Fans leaped for joy on sidewalks, in the streets, even on the cars, shouting, waving and shooting off firecrackers and guns. "I couldn't miss this moment for anything," said Rich Polli of Milwaukee, a Chicago native who returned for Game 5 of the Finals, the Bulls' first chance to win the title. "I've waited 25 years for something like this. I've been through thick and thin with the Bulls, and that makes you appreciate it even more," Polli said. "It's a definite upper for the city. It sheds a new light on the 1991-92 season," said one fan who rushed off to trade high-fives with people in passing cars without giving her name.

A 15-year-old girl was shot during celebrations on the South Side, said Officer Simeon Frost of the Chicago Police Department. The girl was on the street outside her home celebrating with friends when she was shot, apparently by stray gunfire, Frost said.

The girl, whom Frost would not identify, was in good condition today at Mt. Sinai Hospital with a gunshot wound in her thigh. A welcome home rally for the team was scheduled for noon Friday in downtown Grant Park, said Terry Levin, a spokesman for Mayor Richard M. Daley. Levin said the rally would be preceded by a short motorcade.

That doesn't mean nothing was planned for today. Vendors were flooding the city with championship merchandise. And although the championship trophy was still in Los Angeles, another one was on hand for display in the Second - or is that First? - City.

Tiffany's, the jewelry company that designed and created the NBA trophy, made two. One was held aloft by Michael Jordan and company Wednesday night. Tiffany's planned to display the other at its Michigan Avenue store, said vice president Wallace Steiner. For the victory-starved city, the Bulls bring the first championship in any professional sport since the Chicago Bears won the Super Bowl in 1986.

The Chicago Blackhawks of the NHL last won the Stanley Cup in 1961. And for the city's two baseball teams, the drought has been even longer. The White Sox last won the World Series in 1917, and the Cubs took their last series in 1908. Barkeepers began bracing for the Bulls celebration early Wednesday.

"We're taking everything that's not nailed down and putting it in a safe place," Rich Kewitz, owner of Gamekeepers Bar and Grill, said before the game. "Anything that can move, we're taking it and locking it up."

Kewitz said he had received calls from as far afield as Michigan, Wisconsin and Ohio about the possibility of reserving tables at his bar for Wednesday night's game. He turned them all down. "To reserve a table would cause a riot," said Kewitz, who had a line of about 70 people waiting outside the door an hour and a half before the start of the game.

Red Kerr's, a sports bar west of downtown owned by the Bulls' first coach, Johnny "Red" Kerr, was filled to overflowing during the game. Few in the audience there saw the last seconds of the game since patrons were leaping, punching the air, trading high-fives and toasting each other. "You can't beat this!" patron David Tickner shouted over chants of "We're Number One!" Polli looked forward to more titles. "They're a young team, they're very well-coached. This is something they've been building for for a long time, and I think that they can do it again. And again after that," he said.

**Career Snapshot
Three Championship Seasons**

42   AP Editions

1991

The Chicago Bulls' Michael Jordan, left, guards the Los Angeles Lakers Earvin "Magic" Johnson during the first quarter of Game 2 in the NBA Finals, in Chicago, June 5, 1991. (AP Photo/John Swart)

Chicago Bulls Michael Jordan, left, gets a pat from teammate Scottie Pippen during third quarter action against the Los Angeles Lakers. The Bulls beat the Lakers 107-86 to tie the NBA Championship series at one game each in Chicago, June 6, 1991. (AP Photo/John Swart)

Chicago Bulls Michael Jordan raises his arms in celebration with other players on the Bulls bench after defeating the Los Angeles Lakers 97-82 in game four of the NBA finals at the Forum in Inglewood, California, June 9, 1991. (AP Photo/Reed Saxon)

1992

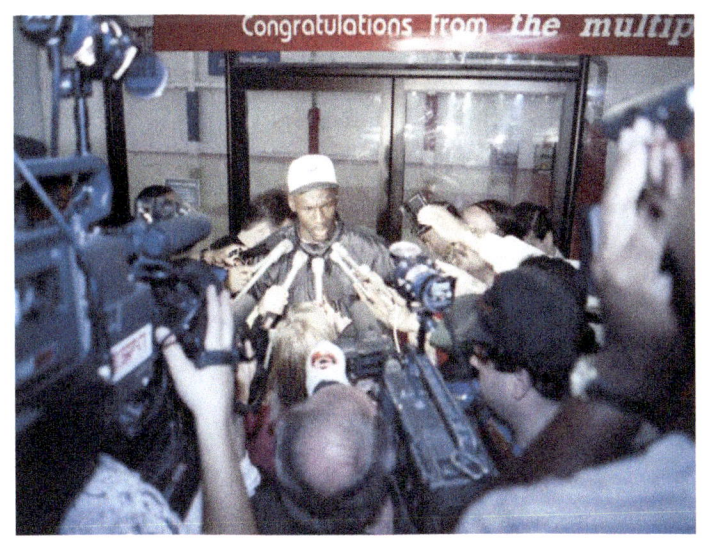

The Chicago Bulls' Michael Jordan is swarmed by reporters as the team practices at the Multiplex in Deerfield, Ill., on, June 1, 1992. (AP Photo/Barry Jarvinen)

Chicago Bulls' Michael Jordan (23) shoots over the Portland Trail Blazers' Clyde Drexler (22) during the Bulls' 122-89 victory in Game 1 of the NBA Finals in Chicago, June 3, 1992. (AP Photo/Fred Jewell)

1993

The Chicago Bulls Michael Jordan, center, slips between the Phoenix Suns Kevin Johnson, left, and Dan Majerle during the first quarter of Game 2 in the NBA Finals in Phoenix, June 11, 1993. (AP Photo/Jeff Robbins)

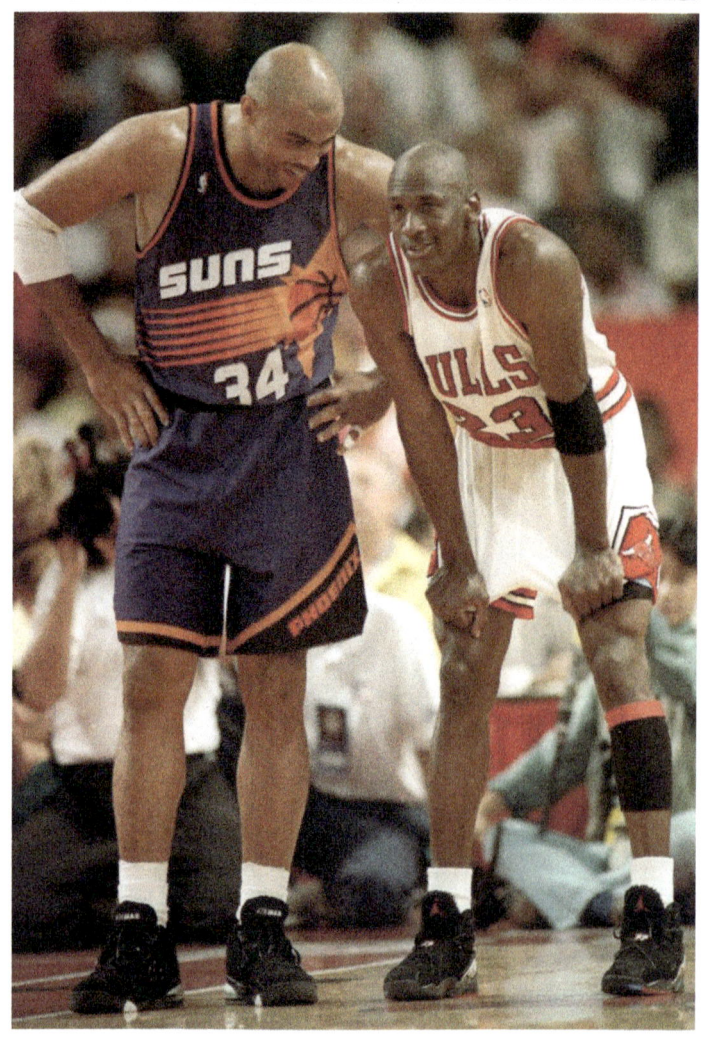

Phoenix Suns' Charles Barkley chats with Chicago Bulls' Michael Jordan during the closing moments of Game 5 in the NBA Finals at the Chicago Stadium, June 18, 1993. (AP Photo/John Swart)

The Chicago Bulls' Michael Jordan gets doused with champagne by teammate Scottie Pippen, right, as he holds the NBA Trophy following their 99-98 win over the Phoenix Suns to win their third straight NBA title, in Phoenix, June 20, 1993. (AP Photo/Scott Troyanos)

3

The Dream Team Legacy

Big Expectations
July 9, 1992
By Jim Irwin

"When we won the championships of Africa we said we wanted to play the U.S.A. because they're the most powerful team in the world," Coach Vitorino Cunha said. "Our goal is to lose between 30, 35, 40 points, no more."

The Angolan team, in Flint for exhibition games, drew the United States in the Olympic opener July 26. The Angolans lost 90-83 Wednesday night to Ragnone AAU, a traveling amateur team.

There's not much argument that Team USA, led by retired Los Angeles Laker Magic Johnson and the Chicago Bulls' Michael Jordan, is the best basketball team ever assembled.

Angola, on Africa's southwestern coast, qualified for the Olympics by winning the African zone championship. Team USA qualified by beating six opponents by an average of 51.5 points at the Tournament of the Americas.

"We will probably lose by 50 points, but we will play hard," Angolan point guard Panto Macedo said through a translator, teammate Nelson Sardinha.

Macedo said he looked forward above all to playing against Jordan. Then he grinned and looked down at the Air Jordan basketball shoes on his feet.

The biggest player on the Angolan team is the 6-foot-7, 286-pound center Ivo Alfredo, who started playing basketball just 18 months ago.

During a drill Wednesday, Alfredo got the ball, spun past his man but nearly fell on his back when he clanged a dunk off the front of the rim.

Cunha revealed some of his strategy: "Put pressure on the ball, double team, overload the passing lanes, that is all I can do."

52   AP Editions

The practice was held before about 100 spectators at a community college gymnasium, with no ball rack, no Gatorade, not even a water cooler.

Gustavo Conceicao, head of the Angolan delegation, said the team hopes to play well enough at the Olympics "to become the best representatives" of Africa.

"We know that we don't have a chance," he said

Michael Jordan, left, of the Chicago Bulls and Earvin "Magic" Johnson of the Los Angeles Lakers sport their new uniforms for the 1992 US Olympic Basketball team in Chicago. This is the first time NBA players have been eligible for Olympic play. The two were attending a benefit to raise funds for the Michael Jordon Foundation, September 21, 1991. (AP Photo/Ralf-Finn Hestoft)

The coach expects to lose by at least 30 points and the point guard by 50. Still, the Angolan national basketball team looks forward to playing the Dream Team at the Olympics.

Big Expectations
August 5, 1992
By Jim O'Connell

USA's Michael Jordan (9), Patrick Ewing (6) and Scottie Pippen (8) cheer on teammates during gold medal basketball game against Croatia in Barcelona. (AP Photo/John Gaps)

Good thing Reebok makes a warmup suit with a company logo that easily disappears.

The design of the suit allowed for a compromise Tuesday between the U.S. Olympic Committee and members of the U.S. basketball team who are under contract to Nike and who said they wouldn't wear a suit by a rival sponsor.

Under the compromise, the players agreed to wear the two-piece Reebok suits but with the collar open - covering the Reebok logo, on the right shoulder.

"Most of the guys are pleased," said Michael Jordan, a Nike spokesman and the most outspoken of the players about refusing to wear the suit.

The jacket is white, with a blue field of white stars on the right sleeve and bold red and white stripes and the USA logo across the bottom.

"In the event the men's basketball team wins a medal, all members will appear on the medal platform in the uniform issued by the United States Olympic Committee," USA Basketball president Dave Gavitt said in a statement.

"Some players may choose to wear the awards suit in a manner that does not reveal any commercial identification. However, in no instance will the uniform be defaced or covered by any other material."

Hours later the Dream Team beat Puerto Rico 115-77 in the quarterfinals to move one step closer to the gold medal.

The controversy began when Nike representatives Jordan and Charles Barkley said they wouldn't wear Reebok suits during the ceremony out of allegiance to the company that pays them millions of dollars to endorse products.

Reebok has a contract with the USOC saying that all medal winners will wear their suits during the medal presentation ceremonies. USOC officials say money received from Reebok goes to support thousands of athletes in training.

In addition, U.S. athletes sign a form saying they will abide by USOC rules - including the one that says medal winners will wear apparel supplied by the USOC at awards ceremonies.

The USOC threatened to stop any player who refused to wear the suit from attending the ceremony, though the player still would have received the medal.

The controversy threatened to hurt the team's image, making personal profit a larger issue than being part of the 600-plus member U.S. Olympic team.

Calls placed after business hours Tuesday to Stoughton, Mass.-based Reebok weren't immediately returned.

Nike has said it doesn't care whether the players wear Reebok suits.

"If we thought ceremonial gear was important, we would have bought it. We don't care. But Michael does what he wants to do," Nike representative Liz Dolan told New York Newsday.

Players seemed happy with the compromise.

"I'll wear it however they tell me to wear it," Barkley said.

"I think everybody will wear the suit and we'll go out and finish this thing with class," said Karl Malone, who wears shoes from LA Gear.

Global Currency
August 8, 1992
By Arnie Stapleton

Michael Jordan, left, and Earvin "Magic" Johnson share a light moment during the U.S. basketball team's first news conference after arriving for the Olympic game in Barcelona, July 25, 1992. (AP Photo/Susan Regan)

You want a global currency? Try the Dream Team.

From bootlegged pins to officially licensed caps and T-shirts, Michael, Magic & Co. are prime barter for the international crowds packing Barcelona's Plaza Espanya.

"Dream Team is recognized by all at first sight," entrepreneur Mike Jackson of San Francisco said Saturday as dozens of people crowded around to gawk over his Team USA pins, basketball cards and key chains.

"The people here are not buying for the quality. It's beautiful to them even if it's cheap-looking," he said.

"All the people talk about getting something with Dream Team on it," said Maria Angeles, 20, of Barcelona. "These guys - Michael Jordan, Magic Johnson, Bird and Barkley - they ARE the Olympics.

"I tried to get a pin, but everybody wants $50."

Jim Parsons of Milton-Freewater, Ore., turned his Team USA baseball cap backwards so that nobody would try to trade for it.

One man wanted a pin with caricatures of all the U.S. players, but was aghast at Jackson's price - $30 or tickets to Saturday night's track and field finals. Jackson asked where the man was from.

"Luxembourg? Well, they don't have them in Luxembourg. I'll sell you a package of cards for 600 pesetas, though."

For roughly $6, Jackson handed the man a package of SkyBox International's Team USA cards that retail back home for $1 a pack.

"What are they going to do?" Jackson said. "I tell them, 'Either you pay my price or you go home with just a memory.' "

MAIL CALL: The U.S. Post Office says it delivered more than 32,000 post cards to U.S. athletes in Barcelona as part of its Sign, Seal and Deliver program.

A portion of the proceeds from the cards, addressed to teams and individuals, went to the U.S. Olympic team.

Not surprisingly, the Dream Team got the most - 2,250 cards. Michael Jordan got 800.

Floridians sent the most: 1,000, while Main and Alaska sent the fewest: 10.

The Postal Service said one in three cards was written by children.

FLAG-BEARING FENCER: Five-time Olympic fencer Peter Westbrook of New York will carry the U.S. flag in Sunday's closing ceremonies. Westbrook, who holds a record 12 national championships in the men's sabre, was chosen by U.S. Olympic team captains.

The 40-year-old native of St. Louis, Mo., won a bronze medal at the 1984 Games in Los Angeles, becoming the first American to to medal in the sport in 24 years.

Westbrook has been on every U.S. Summer Olympics team since Montreal in 1976, and has won two golds in five appearances in the Pan American Games. In 1990, he founded the Peter Westbrook Foundation to attract youths to the sport.

POPULAR PRESS GUIDES: The U.S. Olympic Committee has had problems keeping its tables stocked with press guides.

"Everything we put out just gets eaten up. International reporters pick up everything, even if they can't read English," said press officer Richard Wanninger.

A fresh box of 44 U.S. men's basketball guides, for instance, was gone within five minutes Saturday.

"It seems whatever we put out, we've got to go back later in the day and replenish the supply," Wanninger said as a Pizza Hut delivery woman scooped up a women's basketball guide and roller-skated away.

SURVEY SAYS: One hundred athletes at the Barcelona Olympics were asked the following question: For what do you compete at the Olympics?

Sixty-eight said for their country, followed by: for their dignity; their living; and their social status. When asked for whom did they compete, 83 said "for myself." Other answers were for: my family; my partner; and my coach.

Tough Act to Follow
July 30, 1994
By Bill Barnard

USA World Championship Basketball Team coach Don Nelson of the Golden State Warriors shares a light moment with Shaquille O'Neill of the Orlando Magic as the team poses for a group photo in Chicago, July 20, 1994. (AP Photo/Charles Bennett)

The toughest competition for the United States at the World Championship of Basketball won't be Croatia, Russia, Canada or Puerto Rico.

The toughest competition will be a memory, or more properly, a dream.

Dream Team II, as it's known, has more than enough NBA talent to win the tournament. Coach Don Nelson, from the old school of coaches who usually won't say more than they have to, has already guaranteed victory in the 16-team event, which starts Thursday with the Americans playing Spain.

But even if Dream Team II is too good for the rest of the world, it will inevitably be compared to its predecessor, the original Dream Team of Magic Johnson, Larry Bird, Michael Jordan, Charles Barkley and Scottie Pippen.

The most important numbers during the 10-day run of the World Championship, in fact, might not be the outcomes of games, but the margins of victory. After all, Dream Team I won the Olympics by an average margin of 44 points.

"There's no pressure to win at a certain margin," Nelson says. "The pressure is to play well and win, and I think we're going to do that."

But no one doubts that the comparisons to Dream Team I will be constant and merciless.

"The comparisons started before we even got here," forward Dominique Wilkins said at training camp in Chicago. "They will look at us very hard, maybe harder than the first team, because they are looking at us to do what they did and more. We've got a reputation to uphold."

Nelson, chronically short of big men during his NBA coaching career, is practically giddy over the wealth of talent at his disposal. He promises numerous starting lineup changes to give his charges playing time, if not in every game, at least throughout the tournament.

"We know and everyone else knows it's hard to play 12 guys in a game," Nelson said. "That's just too many. Chuck Daly started different guys every night, and I think it worked out to let everyone play."

In an exhibition against Germany on Tuesday night, Nelson started a relatively small lineup of Kevin Johnson and Reggie Miller at guards, Dan Majerle and Larry Johnson at forwards, and Alonzo Mourning at center. But that group was designed more to keep the local fans in Charlotte happy than anything else.

Dream Team II is perceived as younger and more brash than the 1992 Olympians, who seem destined to be remembered as supremely talented and savvy, but perhaps over the hill.

The generalizations have a certain ring of truth, but there are exceptions to both. Jordan and Barkley were brash even on a team of gigantic egos, and David Robinson and Pippen were still to reach their peak as NBA stars.

Neither is Dream Team II a bunch of swaggering kids barely out of college. Wilkins, Mark Price and Joe Dumars are past 30 and apologize to no one in knowing how the game is played.

There is no question, however, that Dream Team II has its share of the "I Am King of This Realm" types of players - notably Shaquille O'Neal, Miller, Shawn Kemp, Derrick Coleman and Steve Smith. They will be watched closely to see if they adopt the "team first" approach taken by the 1992 squad.

"I think that team understood how to play together," said Kevin Johnson, who has learned how to share the spotlight in Phoenix with Majerle and Barkley. "They knew how to put their egos in check. They knew how to win, and I think that's something we have to develp here."

Majerle and Mourning have a special incentive to do well in Canada. Majerle was a member of the 1988 Olympic team of collegians that lost to the Soviet Union, and Mourning was on the World Championship team that lost in Argentina in 1990.

"I still have strong feelings about not winning the gold medal the last time around," Mourning said. "I don't think a lot of people realize I was a member of that team. But, hey, I'm representing my country, and that's what it's all about. We definitely have the upper hand in that we have a dedicated group of guys who are serious to win the gold medal. I truly think this team will be embraced by the American public because anyone represening their country is going to be counted on to bring home the big medal."

Bringing home the gold could be even easier than it was for the 1992 team because the competition won't be as stiff.

Absent from Canada will be four of the best foreign players from the 1992 Olympics - Drazen Petrovic of silver medal-winning Croatia, Detlef Schrempf of Germany, Sarunas Marciulionis of bronze medal-winning Lithuania, and Alexander Volkov of Russia. Petrovic was killed in a car accident last year, Lithuania lost in the European qualifying tournament and Schrempf and Volkov chose not to play.

Croatia, with current and former NBA players Toni Kukoc, Dino Radja and Stojan Vrankovic, is a heavy favorite to win silver, but Petrovic was one of the few foreign players not intimidated by the U.S. team in 1992.

"I think Croatia will be the best opponent," Nelson said, "but I'm not 100 percent sure of that. You can be surprised who shows up in the international game."

Nelson said that while the Americans appear to be far ahead of the world now that the United States is using NBA players, the days when college stars could carry the weight in international competition are over.

"The team that lost in Argentina four years ago had some terrific college players like Mourning, Billy Owens and Kenny Anderson, but they were lucky to win the bronze medal," the coach said. "The world caught up to our college players."

Still, Nelson, said, Dream Team II has to look at itself as a group of "young guys who haven't won anything yet. Until we have that gold medal around our necks, we have to win by as much as we can. We're not taking anything for granted. We're working hard to get ready."

"We should beat anybody we play handily, so we just have to prepare ourselves to play anyone that comes along. We hope this will be the best experience they've had in their lives."

The Novelty is Gone
July 8, 1996
By Chris Sheridan

At least Charles Barkley is back. That should make things a little bit interesting.

Now that the Dream Team is no longer an Olympic novelty, the sideshow that threatened to overshadow the Barcelona Games, the only suspense going into Atlanta will be whether the U.S. men's basketball team draws the interest it did in '92.

Back then, the mere idea was astonishing. Michael Jordan, Larry Bird, Magic Johnson and Barkley on the same team? With America's professionals in the Olympics for the first time, the only thing more thrilling than being routed by the Dream Team was having photos taken with its stars afterwards.

This time around, Jordan, Bird and Magic won't be back, Seattle's Shawn Kemp was left off the team and Dennis Rodman wasn't even considered. The names on the new roster _ including six Olympic veterans _ lack much of the charisma and mythical greatness of the '92 team.

So what's there to look forward to?

Mitch Richmond yawning gimme 3-pointers from a shorter 3-point line, David Robinson posting up some awestruck Argentinian and John Stockton saying, "I'm just gonna go play."

"You're playing in your country, you're representing the United States and you're here, where your fans can come and see you," said Karl Malone, a veteran of the '92 team. "That U.S. pride is going to come on now. I'm not going into it like it's a drag or something."

Dream Team III coach Lenny Wilkens, center, talks to the U.S. Olympic team before its game against Greek Olympic team at the RCA Dome in Indianapolis, July 14, 1996. (AP Photo/Phil Meyers)

The competition from the rest of the world is at least a decade away from being anything near truly challenging, and each blowout will be followed two days later by another. That won't keep the games out of prime time, though, since NBC dictated that four of the five U.S. men's basketball games begin at 10 p.m. EDT, the other at 7 p.m. on a Sunday.

"This is what the world wants," said Craig Miller, spokesman for USA Basketball. "The television ratings four years ago showed it."

One redeeming factor in the excitement department is Barkley, who was chosen over Kemp for one of the final two spots.

While he won't be holding court on the city streets the way he did in Barcelona, Barkley will be reunited with Erlander Coimbra, the skinny Angolan player who gained fame for absorbing a nasty elbow from Barkley in the tournament's opening game.

Barkley was roundly criticized back home, and indeed the team's 32-point average victory margin was as much a cause for American shame as American pride.

Maintaining a distinction between pride and offensiveness is one of the biggest concerns for USA Basketball, the governing body that was criticized for the showboating antics of Dream Team II when it won the 1994 world championship.

"We want character, not characters," USA Basketball president C.M. Newton said last summer when the first 10 members of the new team were chosen.

Dream Team III is a mix of old and new.

Barkley, Malone, Stockton, Scottie Pippen and David Robinson return from the 1992 team; Reggie Miller and Shaquille O'Neal were on the '94 team; and Anfernee Hardaway, Grant Hill, Hakeem Olajuwon, Richmond and Glenn Robinson are first-time Dream Teamers.

Robinson and Richmond also played on the 1988 team, a collegiate squad that brought home a disappointing bronze medal.

Before beating up on the world, the team that averaged more than 117 points a game in '92 will embark on a national tour that includes stops in Phoenix, Indianapolis, Auburn Hills, Mich., and Salt Lake City and a three-day stop in Orlando.

"The glitz and glamour, all of that is OK, but I kind of like being here at home and going to Orlando and Phoenix and Utah and all those places," Malone said. "I'd rather do that. We don't have to take a 10-12 hour flight to get places."

The Dream Team is serious business to merchandisers and advertisers, who have had T-shirts and hats on the shelves for months, Dream Team-theme ads on the air for weeks and Olajuwon's picture on potato-chip packages.

The continuing commercialism will be huge.

"We're in our own country now, and I think it will be a bigger deal here," Malone said. "If we would have gone back to Barcelona, maybe it wouldn't be a bigger deal, but hey, we're playing in the United States."

And this time, there should be no logo controversy among the multimillionaire Olympians.

In 1992, some players with Nike shoe contracts spread word that they wouldn't appear on the medal stand wearing warmups bearing the Reebok logo. In a compromise, and one that outraged many, Johnson, Jordan and others draped American flags over the offending logo on their warmups.

No such flap is expected this time, since Champion Sports, not Nike or Reebok, will have its name on the official warmups. The U.S. team also changed its practice of awarding a shoe contract, knowing that the players would refuse to wear rival brands.

The Dream Team won't be the only team in Atlanta playing with NBA stars.

Croatia features Toni Kukoc of the Chicago Bulls, Dino Radja of the Boston Celtics and Zan Tabak of the Toronto Raptors. Lithuania has Sarunas Marciulionis of the Denver Nuggets and Arvydas Sabonis of the Portland Trail Blazers. Yugoslavia has Vlade Divac of the Los Angeles Lakers and Sasha Danilovic of the Miami Heat.

The United States is grouped in Pool A with Angola, Argentina, China, Croatia and Lithuania. Pool B consists of Australia, Brazil, Greece, Puerto Rico, South Korea and Yugoslavia.

No Contest
July 29, 1996
By Mike Nadel

If there ever was a debate, Michael Jordan ended it in a matter of seconds.

"Dream Team I. Easy."

Jordan, brought to Atlanta for a day by one of his corporate sponsors, said that the 1992 U.S. Olympic men's basketball team _ the first to use pros instead of collegians _ was superior to the current squad.

Nevertheless, the NBA's career scoring-average leader believes that criticism of the current team is unwarranted.

"These guys are up-and-coming stars. Everyone's trying to compare them to mature players in '92," Jordan said. "It's unfair."

Five of Jordan's Barcelona teammates _ Scottie Pippen, Charles Barkley, Karl Malone, John Stockton and David Robinson _ also are on the current Dream Team. The others who played with Jordan four years ago were Larry Bird, Magic Johnson, Patrick Ewing, Clyde Drexler, Chris Mullin and Christian Laettner. The team won its eight games by an average of 44 points.

This team, featuring Shaquille O'Neal, Penny Hardaway, Grant Hill, Hakeem Olajuwon, Reggie Miller, Gary Payton and Mitch Richmond, didn't play up to expectations early in the tournament. But it still goes into the medal round with a 5-0 record and an average victory margin of 35 points.

Dream Team members, from left: David Robinson, Scottie Pipen, Mitch Richmond, Reggie Miller, Gary Payton and Shaquille O'Neal, listen to the national anthem during medal ceremonies for men's basketball at the Centennial Summer Olympic Games in Atlanta, August 3, 1996. (AP Photo/Eric Draper)

"These guys are going to be great players for years to come," Jordan said. "They seem as dominant as ever, which I expected."

He doesn't regret passing up a shot at a third gold medal to go with those he won in 1992 and 1984. After leading the Bulls to the NBA title last season, Jordan is content to "watch the Olympics from afar."

Sara Lee, the parent company of several products Jordan endorses, wanted to keep the visit by one of the world's most recognizable figures under wraps. So they gave him an alias _ "Frank Gordon" _ and invited only a few members of the media to Monday's briefing.

"I'm happy they brought me in for a day," Jordan said. "That's all I needed, a day. Get the taste of the Olympic experience, and then get back to Chicago and watch the rest of it on TV."

Jordan addressed several subjects besides the Dream Team:

- On the bomb that killed one woman and injured more than 100 early Saturday at Centennial Olympic Park: "You think about where our society is ... with terrorists and all the opportunities that people have to make a point, the anger that these individuals must have. I was very frightened by it. My wife was supposed to come, but she chickened out. It's sad that we can't celebrate without worrying."

- On the importance of the Bulls signing Dennis Rodman: "It could be a crucial point to put us further ahead of the NBA. I'm not saying we can't win without him, but it clearly makes us a better team to have him."

- On O'Neal leaving Orlando, the Bulls' main Eastern Conference rival, for Los Angeles: "Orlando is going to go through an identity crisis. Penny is going to be maybe even better, but other players are going to be exposed without the double-teaming of Shaq _ especially Dennis Scott and Horace (Grant)."

- On the escalation of NBA salaries, including Jordan getting at least $25 million next season, O'Neal signing for $120 million over seven years and many lesser players becoming overnight multimillionaires: "Evidently, it's affordable, or else they wouldn't pay it. I think the owners are a little bit smarter than that, to give out money they can't make. So I know they've made it."

4

Drugs, Gambling, Death and Baseball

Drug Dealer
October 17, 1992
By Paul A. Driscoll

Picture of Michael Jordon in 1991. (AP Photo/Nick Ut)

Basketball star Michael Jordan is refusing to discuss a newspaper story that quoted him as saying he had not publicly told the truth about the purpose of a $57,000 check he wrote to a convicted drug dealer.

The Chicago Sun-Times reported Friday that Jordan admitted he lost the money gambling last year while his Chicago Bulls teammates were visiting President Bush.

Jordan has insisted publicly that the money was a loan to help the drug dealer build a golf driving range.

"The story is an allegation from the Sun-Times," Jordan said Friday at a news conference. "It's not something I gave them."

The news conference was called to announce that he and Nike Inc. were donating $100,000 each to a fund for sports and other extracurricular activities at Chicago high schools. Jordan said the news conference "isn't the proper arena" to discuss the gambling story.

The dealer, James "Slim" Bouler, faces a trial Tuesday in U.S. District Court in Charlotte, N.C., on charges of laundering money for a cocaine ring. Jordan is listed in court documents as a subpoenaed defense witness.

"I will show up. I won't run, and I'll answer the questions that are put to me," Jordan said. He said his lawyer told him not to elaborate on the allegations.

Jordan didn't deny the accuracy of the Sun-Times story, which quoted him as saying he initially put out a false story about the money because he was embarrassed.

The prosecution alleges the check was a payoff for a golf gambling debt he incurred in October 1991, while his teammates were visiting the White House to celebrate their National Basketball Association championship. Jordan isn't under criminal investigation, but the NBA warned him earlier this year to be more careful about his associations.

Thank You
August 19, 1993
By Jim Litke

Michael Jordan thanked supporters for their sympathy following his father's slaying, and criticized some media speculation that the death might be linked with shady business deals or his own gambling.

"The many kind words and thoughtful prayers have lifted our spirits through difficult times," the professional basketball star said in a statement issued by his Washington lawyer, David Falk. "I also want to express my appreciation to the local, state and federal law enforcement officers for their efforts."

Jordan said he always believed that James Jordan's death was a random act of violence and rebuked news reports that it might be connected with family misdeeds.

James Jordan, father of Chicago Bulls' Michael Jordan is shown in this photo, 1993. (AP Photo/Tim Boyle)

Chicago Bulls' Michael Jordan talks to reporters at the Rose Elder Invitational pro-am golf tournament. Jordan, in his first public appearance since the slaying of his father, said he and his family were coping well in the aftermath of the trauma in Leesburg, Virginia, August 21, 1993. (AP Photo/Wilfredo Lee)

"I was outraged when this speculation continued even after the arrests of the alleged murderers," Jordan said. "These totally unsubstantiated reports reflect a complete lack of sensitivity to basic human decency."

Authorities have charged two 18-year-olds from North Carolina, Larry Martin Demery and Daniel Andre Green, in James Jordan's death, saying the two planned to rob someone and Jordan stumbled into their path.

He was shot to death after stopping his Lexus on a state highway to rest early on July 23 during a trip to Charlotte.

"When James Jordan was murdered, I lost my Dad," Jordan said. "I also lost my best friend. I am trying to deal with the overwhelming feelings of loss and grief in a way that would make my Dad proud.

"I simply cannot comprehend how others could intentionally pour salt in my open wound by insinuating that faults and mistakes in my life are in some way connected to my father's death."

Jordan said most news accounts have been fair. "Unfortunately, a few engaged in baseless speculation and sensationalism," he added.

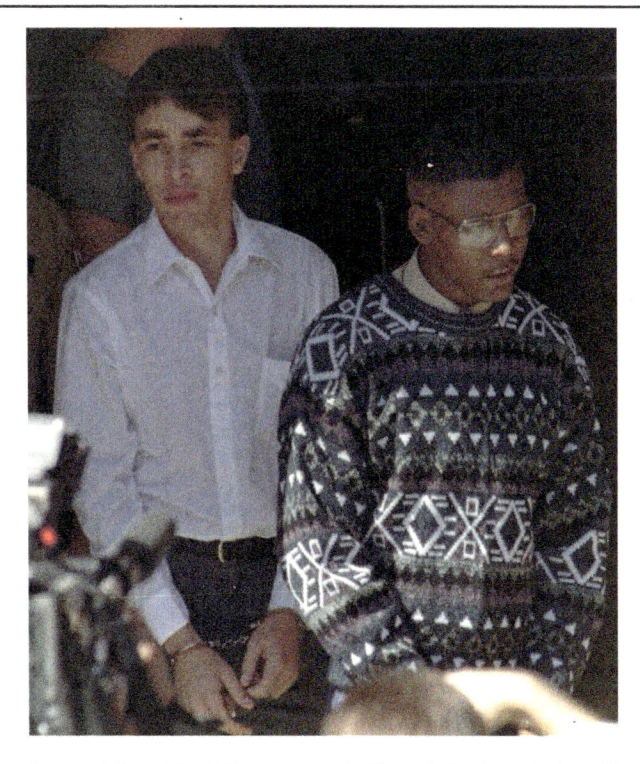

Larry Demery, left, and Daniel Green, charged with murdering James Jordan, father of NBA star Michael Jordan, leave the courthouse in Lumberton, N.C., October 5, 1993. (AP Photo/Jim Bounds)

Retiring
October 6, 1993
By Jim Litke

Michael Jordan, basketball's greatest player, announced today that he was retiring after nine seasons in the NBA, saying he "had reached the pinnacle of my career" and had nothing else to prove.

In a news conference at the Chicago Bulls' training center, Jordan said the murder of his father, James, in July made him realize that "it can be taken away from you at any time."

"I guess the biggest gratification - I am a very positive person - I can get out of my father not being here today is, that he saw my last baseball game. It is something that we have talked about a lot," Jordan said.

The startling announcement by basketball's greatest player leaves the Chicago Bulls without their seven-time scoring champion, the NBA without its glitziest attraction, and millions of fans without the hero who redefined standards of excellence.

Jordan's departure at the top of his game occurred during a year of unprecedented success - and personal tragedy. He led his Chicago Bulls to a third-straight NBA championship, but also suffered the loss of his father, who was shot and killed. The 30-year-old superstar, whose salary and endorsements bring him more than $50 million a year, also was dogged by reports of excessive gambling.

But Jordan left open the possibility of returning to the game.

"Would I ever unretire? I don't know. I think the word 'retire' means you can do whatever you want, and maybe someday down the road, that's what I'll desire to do," he said.

Jordan had three years left on his $4 million-a-year contract.

Members of the Chicago Bulls, along with coach Phil Jackson, right, and general manager Jerry Krause, seated at center, watch as Michael Jordan announces his retirement from basketball and the Bulls at Berto Center in Deerfield, Ill., October 6, 1993. (AP Photo/Mark Elias)

Jordan's fame extended far beyond Chicago and the NBA. At last year's Barcelona Olympics, he was treated more like a potentate or rock star. In China, he is the most celebrated figure apart from Mao Tse-tung - this in a country where basketball is not even the most popular sport.

His departure follows the retirement last year of Larry Bird and Magic Johnson, dealing the NBA an incalculable loss.
With his slithering drives through the lane, airborne slams and radar 3-point shots - always with his tongue hanging out - Jordan played the game like no other.

"In my mind, he's the greatest player who ever played the game, and the most special athlete I've had the pleasure of watching," said Tom Wilson, president of the Detroit Pistons.

Charles Barkley, the Phoenix Suns MVP who played with Jordan on the Dream Team at Barcelona and against him in last season's NBA finals, said: "Michael Jordan is the only person in this entire world that I've ever met who is as competitive as I am. That's why I'll miss playing against him."

Jordan's announcement comes one day after a North Carolina prosecutor said he will seek the death penalty for the two 18-year-olds accused of killing James Jordan, who was shot during a robbery July 23 as he napped in his luxury car along a highway.

In recent years, Jordan admitted losing large bets to a convicted North Carolina drug dealer in 1991. A book earlier this year accused him of losing more than $1 million in golf bets.

The same week the book came out, Jordan gambled with his father at an Atlantic City, N.J., casino the night before a playoff game with the New York Knicks.

The NBA said Jordan violated no laws or rules, but Stern said last month that Jordan's gambling is "not a closed subject with us."

Jordan began his NBA career in 1984 after being named college player of the year at the University of North Carolina in both 1983 and '84.

He led the Bulls to their first NBA title in 1991, and the following year the Bulls became only the second NBA team in more than 20 years to win back-to-back championships. They won their third consecutive title last season.

In 1984, before his rookie season, he was the star as the U.S. Olympic basketball team went unbeaten at the Los Angeles Games and won the gold medal.

Jordan was back in 1992 when the Olympics allowed professionals into basketball. He, Johnson, Bird and others made up the Dream Team that easily won the gold at Barcelona.

Retired Chicago Bulls' star Michael Jordan speaks to the crowd as he stands with the Bulls' three championship trophies following presentation of the 1993 NBA Championship rings prior to the Bulls home opener against the Miami Heat at Chicago Stadium, November 6, 1993. (AP Photo/Ralf-Finn Hestoft)

New Field
February 13, 1994
By Rick Gano

From the air to the outfield, from high tops to cleats, Michael Jordan has a new job and a new pair of shoes.

But don't expect the career change to ground his appeal with Madison Avenue.

"We want a positive role model in addition to awareness, and Michael's got that whether he plays baseball or doesn't," said Margaret Riley, a spokeswoman for High Grade Food Products, the Southfield, Mich., company that produces Ball Park Franks.

"We like baseball because we have a product named after it," she said. "But because he's deciding to play baseball, that doesn't mean we're changing anything. But it's a nice tie-in."

Instead of finding his way to the basket, Jordan, the ultimate pitchman, now must figure how to hit 90-mph pitches. And one New York talent agent says "the only down side would be if he embarrassed himself; that's the one danger in this."

Marty Blackman, who works for a firm that matches advertising and sports figures, said: "If the media plays it up and he hits .055 and makes 10 errors every day, that is harmful.

Michael Jordan swings a weighted bat while waiting for his turn in the batting cage during his first day of spring training with the Chicago White Sox, in Sarasota, Florida, February 2, 1994. (AP Photo/John Swart)

Chicago White Sox's Michael Jordan, formerly of the NBA Chicago Bulls, loses his cap during batting practice at the Chicago White Sox training camp in Sarasota, Florida, February 15, 1994. (AP Photo/John Swart)

"But looking at the positive side, if he makes it, the roof opens up again. If he's respectable and spends three years in the minors or decides not to spend that kind of time that situation is still a boom for all of his advertisers. ... He will only lose if it is a disaster."

David Burns, who runs a sports celebrity service in Chicago, said Jordan's advertising future is set well in advance.

"His agent has been very shrewd," Burns said. "When someone calls to do a commercial, it had better be multiyear and it better have at least $5 million.

"It will be two or three years before Michael will be available for any more advertising contracts. He could make an exception as he did for Gatorade when he signed for 10 years for $18 million."

Burns said Jordan's baseball venture won't diminish his popularity.

"People will love him just as much," Burns said. "They'll admire him for trying."

A sports industry publication estimated that last year Jordan made $17 million or more from product royalties and commercial appearances for Nike.

"There are no specific ad concepts, but I can't imagine there's not some creative genius with something sketched out on a pad somewhere," Nike spokesman Keith Peters said of Jordan and baseball.

Jordan basketball apparel at Nike Town in downtown Chicago is still selling strong, manager Bruce Hochberg said.

He said it's too soon for there to have been any appreciable change in volume since Jordan signed a contract last week with the White Sox.

"The No. 23 (Bulls) jerseys are going very well," Hochberg said. "Sales are very good in every part of Jordan whether he signs with the White Sox or not. Jordan is still Jordan. It's very strong.

Phones at the White Sox offices and those of the Nashville Sounds of the Triple A American Association, where Jordan might be assigned, have been ringing wildly all week since he was invited to spring training.

Rob Gallas, vice president of marketing and broadcasting for the White Sox, said spring training ticket and season ticket sales already were going well because the team won the AL West last season.

"We have noticed the phone calls wrapping up on the switchboards, about 100 calls on spring training. Normally we might get a dozen," Gallas said.

"Michael's specter certainly has increased interest. But we were going to set records anyway."

Chicago White Sox' Michael Jordan takes batting practice before the start of the game against the Chicago Cubs in their annual cross-town classic, April 7, 1994. (AP Photo/Barry Jarvinen)

Some have accused the White Sox of grandstanding by letting the 30-year-old Jordan try out, even though he hasn't played organized baseball since high school.

But Gallas said, for now, the team is taking a cautious approach to pushing No. 45 Jordan the baseball player. It's been four months since No. 23 Jordan, the basketball player, retired after taking the Bulls to three straight NBA titles.

"Everybody is in a big hurry to get licensing merchandise into the market by spring training," Gallas said. "We've been trying to slow people down and let them know we just don't know where it's going. Is it two weeks, two months or two years?"

One Chicago song writer already is trying to market Jordan's baseball experience with a tune titled "Air On My Sox."

"I've got air on my Sox, it's a summertime thing, add to the collection a World Series ring," goes the song, written by Gregg Shipp.

Birmingham Barons' left fielder Michael Jordan, formerly of the NBA Chicago Bulls, shags flies during pre-game warm-ups at the Hoover Metropolitan Stadium prior to the Barons' game against the Knoxville Smokies, August 10, 1994. (AP Photo/Dave Martin)

The Rules of Rhubarb
May 28, 1994
By Ben Walker

Birmingham Barons Michael Jordan is brushed back by a pitch in the third inning of their game against the Chattanooga Lookouts at the Hoover Metropolitan Stadium in Birmingham, Alabama, April 8, 1994. (AP Photo/Dave Martin)

Early April, early innings. Michael Jordan is called out on a close pitch, and he doesn't like it.

He stomps around the batter's box, goes face-to-face with umpire Andy Fletcher, and angrily flings his bat toward the dugout.

Mid-May, middle innings. Jordan is called out - again by Fletcher - for sliding out of the basepath trying to break up a double play. The interference ruling with the bases loaded is a big one, and Birmingham Barons manager Terry Francona goes crazy and gets ejected.

Jordan, however, stays cool. Instead, at the end of the inning, as he runs past the umpire on his way to right field, he stops and calmly says, "Andy, I'm 6-foot-6. I think I can reach the bag from there."

Fletcher patiently points out he doesn't think so, and that's it. No waving arms, no going wild.

"I think the problem early in the season was that Michael didn't know how to argue with an umpire," said Brian King, Fletcher's partner on the two-man Southern League crew. "He's gotten much better at it."

There have been a lot of things for Jordan to learn this year in his quest to become a baseball player, and how to jaw with the ump is one of them. It's not like the NBA, where he got superstar treatment from the officials, it was explained early.

"I told him you can't try to show me up or make a scene every time," Fletcher said. "Then I said something to Terry."

"Andy said there was a problem and that I needed to fix it," Francona said. "I appreciated that. That was the right way to do it, I think, to let the manager deal with a problem with one of his players. I thought Andy and Brian showed a good understanding of the situation."

Next, Francona took aside Jordan.

"I don't really remember what I said. It wasn't much," Francona said. "I think we just talked about umpires and the job they do and dealing with them."

King said he's seen the improvement.

"He uses our names now when he argues. He didn't do that before," he said. "There's nothing wrong with him questioning a call. There's just a right way and a wrong way to do it."

To Jordan, it's how the umpire handles himself that matters.

"I always try to get along with officials," he said. "Sometimes, they won't let you. They build a wall when they won't admit they're wrong. I admit I am wrong, when I am wrong."

"One of the great things about Jake O'Donnell was he could say, 'I blew it.' I can respect a man for that," he said.

O'Donnell, a prominent NBA referee, was a former baseball umpire. In the Southern League, in fact, on a crew with Bill Kunkel.

Jordan, however, was the one admitting a mistake recently. It happened after that play in which he was called out for sliding wide of the baseline.

"I saw the film the next day, and I was out," Jordan said. "That night, I went up and apologized to Fletcher and told him I was wrong."

Marv Wright and Randy Wagner, another Southern League crew, have seen the difference in Jordan's demeanor.

"I called him out on a steal play early this year in Carolina, and he jumped up and was in my face," Wagner said. "I called him out on strikes twice recently and I don't think he liked the calls, but he didn't say anything and went back to the dugout."

Wright said that even if Jordan doesn't hoot on a call, the umpires are sure to hear it from the crowd.

"If he's batting and it's a close pitch and you call it a ball, people think you're just giving it to him because he's Michael Jordan," he said. "But if you call it a strike, they think you're sticking it to him because of who he is."

Wright said there's one thing Jordan quickly picked up.

"Usually, when a player is in his first year, he always calls us 'blue.' As in, 'Hey blue, that pitch was low.'

"But not once has Michael called us 'blue,'" he said. "He's learning our names."

Coming Back?
March 9, 1995
By Mike Nadel

Michael Jordan arrives at the Chicago Bulls' Berto training center. "I'm back," Jordan said in a statement released by his agent, David Falk, confirming that Jordan's first game back will be a nationally televised contest Sunday against the Indianapolis Pacers, March 18, 1995, (AP Photo/Tim Boyle)

Michael Jordan worked out with the Chicago Bulls again today, then left practice without commenting on his future in either basketball or baseball. Bulls coach Phil Jackson said it was his understanding Jordan would soon have an announcement, perhaps as early as today.

"As far as Michael and all the speculation in basketball, we just have to hang tight here and wait to see what goes on," Jackson said after practice.

"I wouldn't say it's a possibility. I wouldn't say anything about probabilities or possibilities. The options are there. It's legal. He's got no other thing to go to now with baseball off. It's a reality. ... But it's still not a reality. So we're not pinning any hopes and we're not trying to throw up a balloon or a kite that's not ready to fly."

Guard B.J. Armstrong said today he wasn't sure what Jordan would do. "I wouldn't be surprised with anything Michael does. He's full of suprises. I won't dare ask him personally. That's none of my business," Armstrong said.

The Chicago Bulls Michael Jordan jokes around at team practice at the Berto Center training facility. Jordan made his return to the NBA Sunday in the 103-96 loss to the Indiana Pacers in Indianapolis, March 20, 1995.

"He's practicing with the second unit. It's not like he's coming in and we're running plays for him. When someone gets tired on the floor, he just steps in. I don't think it's anything he hasn't done before. I just think now it sounds better because baseball is striking."

Bulls captain Scottie Pippen said he would welcome a chance to play with Jordan again.

"I'd be happy to have any of my past teammates back," said Pippen.

The Chicago Bulls Michael Jordan walks away after talking with reporters at the Berto Center training facility, March 20, 1995. (AP Photo/Tim Boyle)

Jordan showed up before practice this morning and was one of the first players on the court, shooting baskets with Toni Kukoc. He was wearing a white sleeveless T-shirt that said "Bulls" on the front in red and black letters.

Jordan also worked out Wednesday, and while he was at the Bulls' Berto Center on Tuesday, it was unclear whether he worked out on his own since the team had no practice that day. But Jackson did say Jordan dropped by and watched some film Tuesday.

Outside the facility, radio talk shows buzzed with questions.

Bulls and White Sox owner Jerry Reinsdorf today offered few clues on Jordan's actions.

"I haven't talked to Michael. I like him with the White Sox or the Bulls. Whatever makes him happy, I'm for," Reinsdorf said today from the owners' baseball meetings in Palm Beach, Fla.

"Michael's been working out with the Bulls for the last two years, there's no significance in that."

Earlier, when asked if he thought Jordan was coming back to basketball, Reinsdorf replied, "Who knows? It could be."

Jordan's agent, David Falk, was out of his Washington office and was not available for comment this morning.

Bulls general manager Jerry Krause and White Sox general manager Ron Schueler both denied knowledge of another impending career change for Jordan.

Krause said Jordan has shot around at the Bulls' training facility many times before. Jordan lives just a mile from the Berto Center.

"When he's home and he needs a workout, the door is always open for him," Krause said.

Schueler said today in Florida that he had no idea what was going on.

"I have nothing," the GM said. "Obviously, the phone has been ringing off the hook for the last 12 hours now but it started with him going to a workout.

"Well, he's been doing that all winter. He practiced with Phoenix, he practiced with Golden State and he practiced with the Bulls.

"I talked to Jerry. If that's his decision to go back, then I respect his decision. He's a pro and he's got to decide what his future is. I'm not here to decide it."

Jordan bolted camp March 2 after the White Sox split their team into players who would compete in exhibition games and those who wouldn't. He cleaned out his locker and flew back to Chicago March 3.

Schueler said before Wednesday's exhibition game against the Detroit Tigers that Jordan has until Saturday to report to the White Sox minor league spring training camp.

"Physicals are Friday," he said. "You have to be on the field Saturday. Since he's been for a physical, he has to be here Saturday."

When asked would Jordan be suspended, fined or released if he doesn't report Saturday, Schueler said, "I'd guess that he'd be retired."

Jordan is technically not due until the minor league camp gets under way. Players not competing in exhibitions, which the striking union has declared are replacement games, have been allowed to work out. But they had to move their belongings into the minor league clubhouse and conduct drills without the major league staff.

NBA spokesman John Maroon said today there would be no league restrictions to Jordan returning to the Bulls.

"The only thing the league is concerned about is that there is a spot on the roster. In the first year it would have required a vote by the board of governors. But now no. Now it's the club's call," Maroon said.

Jordan played at Double-A Birmingham last season, hitting just .202 with 51 RBIs, three homers and 30 stolen bases. He also competed in the Arizona Fall League and had hoped to move up to Triple-A this season, but his departure last week left his future unclear.

Jordan had made it known before camp opened in mid-February he did not want to get caught in the middle of labor strife and would not be a replacement player.

Jordan retired from the Bulls in October 1993 after a nine-year career in which he averaged 32.3 points. He was a three-time MVP in the NBA.

The Bulls retired his number last November and unveiled a statue of him outside their new home at the United Center.

Adjusting the Strategy
March 10, 1995
By Skip Wollenberg

Michael Jordan's decision to quit baseball is driving advertisers to juggle their plans for getting commercial mileage out of the highest-paid advertising spokesman in sports.

Nike Inc. said Friday it will shelve a commercial that debuted only a week ago saluting the basketball superstar's efforts to reach the big leagues in baseball. But Gatorade Co. accelerated the debut of its new ad featuring Jordan on a mythical but suddenly apt search for the meaning of life.

Sneaker marketer Nike hired film director Spike Lee and recruited some of baseball's biggest names including Ken Griffey Jr. and Hall of Famers Stan Musial and Willie Mays for the ad in which they watched Jordan practice.

"He's trying," the sports celebrities said in the spot, aimed at reinforcing Nike's advertising theme "Just Do It."

But Nike spokesman Tom Feuer said the company decided to shelve the ad after Jordan said he was quitting baseball because it was no longer relevant.

Chicago Bulls Guard Michael Jordan answers questions during a post-game news conference, Marc 24, 1995. (AP Photo/Roberto Borea)

Feuer said the commercial is getting plenty of exposure anyway in news accounts of the possibility that Jordan will soon resume his basketball career with the Chicago Bulls. "It hasn't been a waste of money," he said.

The fast-breaking developments involving Jordan drove Gatorade to capitalize on the chance for wider exposure of its new ad.

Bill Schmidt, a top marketing executive for the sports drink, said the company would run the ad on Sunday's NBA broadcasts rather than hold off until April as earlier planned.

The ad was shot three weeks ago and showed Jordan running through the desert and into the mountains to a temple where he meets a guru who recognizes that he has come to discover the meaning of life.

"Life is a sport, drink it up," the guru says.

"Yeah, that's what I figured," Jordan replies.

Michael Jordan 89

Jordan makes an estimated $31 million a year from commercials and other endorsement deals, which Sports Marketing Letter publisher Brian Murphy says is more than twice the take of any other sports figure.

Among his other deals are commercial contracts for McDonald's, Wheaties, Ball Park Franks and Hanes underwear.

Chicago Bulls' Michael Jordan practices his blind free throw as he warms up early on March 19, 1995. (AP Photo/Michael Conroy)

"It doesn't affect our plans," said Kathryn Newton, a spokeswoman for General Mills Inc. in Minneapolis which has been running a commercial since last fall with Jordan endrosing the new taste formulation for Wheaties.

Jordan's endorsement appeal appeared to have been little affected by his surprise decision in the fall of 1993 to retire after leading the Chicago Bulls to three consecutive NBA championships. He began his brief pro baseball career the next spring in the minor league system of the Chicago White Sox. Some of the companies who had him under contract capitalized on the career switch to baseball in commercials.

Ball Park Franks, for example, poked fun at the media hysteria over it with an ad in which speculation erupted that he was going to buy a baseball stadium when someone overheard his plan to by a "Ball Park." He wound up buying a hot dog.

Last fall, Hanes featured Jordan in a commercial in which he stood in a ballpark in street clothes and noted he had changed teams and sports.

"Change is good, as long as it's Hanes," he said in the ad that showed the variety of colors and styles of its underwear.

Chicago Bulls Michael Jordan, right, answers reporters' questions as he leaves practice at the United Center, March 23, 1995. (AP Photo/Tim Boyle)

Sidney Falken, director of marketing for Hanes, said Jordan's real appeal is his likability and said that is unaffected by what sport he plays.

"We haven't emphasized his performance as an athlete. Our use of him has related to his charm and personality... He brings a lot to whatever he decides to do," she said.

Nike had been hoping to use the commercial with Jordan practicing baseball through the spring. The ad, shot in November, reunited Jordan with Lee in his role as a fervent fan of Jordan. They appeared in several "Spike and Mike" ads for Nike between 1988 and 1990.

"Whatever makes Michael happy makes Nike happy," Feuer said. "I am sure we will do some new spots. He's like Joe Dimaggio _ a cultural icon bigger than the environment that immediately surrounds him."

Guilty Verdict
April 27, 1995
By Estes Thompson

A 19-year-old man pleaded guilty Thursday to first-degree murder in the death of basketball superstar Michael Jordan's father and agreed to testify against his co-defendant.

Larry Martin Demery, who still could be sentenced to death, also pleaded guilty to robbery, weapons violations and other charges in two other robberies.

Demery agreed to testify against 20-year-old Daniel Green in the death of James Jordan.

Demery faces a minimum sentence of life in prison on the first-degree murder charge. In entering the plea, he said understood that the maximum penalty was death.

Judge Gregory Weeks agreed that Demery's sentencing will be delayed until after Green's trial.

Demery was charged with first-degree murder, armed robbery and conspiracy in the July 23, 1993, slaying of Jordan.

Jordan was shot as he napped in his car on the shoulder of an isolated highway south of town. He had been traveling from Wilmington, where the Jordans once lived, to Charlotte where they made their home.

Larry Martin Demery, who has pleaded guilty to murdering and robbing James Jordan, father of Michael Jordan, arrives at the courthouse in Lumberton, N.C. He agreed to testify in the Daniel Green murder trial. Green is also charged with killing Jordan, January 25, 1996, (AP Photo/Bob Jordan)

The plea came as Michael Jordan was in Charlotte preparing to lead the Chicago Bulls into the NBA playoffs just a few weeks after his return to basketball.

When he walked away at the pinnacle of his career in October 1993, he spoke of an "overwhelming feeling of grief and loss" after the death of the man he considered his greatest influence and closest friend.

James Jordan died just a month after watching his son lead the Bulls to a third NBA title. Michael Jordan said his decision to retire had been in the making before his father's murder, "but I think what it made me realize is how short life is."

After a brief stint in minor league baseball, he rejoined the team earlier this year. He left his No. 23 jersey hanging in the rafters at the Bulls' home arena, saying it was the last number his father had seen him wear. Instead, he wears the No. 45 he wore as an outfielder for the Double-A Birmingham Barons.

The plea from Demery came just a few weeks before he had been scheduled for trial on charges of first-degree murder, robbery and conspiracy.

He had pleaded innocent, but told police in August 1993 that he helped dispose of Jordan's body. Demery's defense lawyers fought to keep the statement out of evidence, but lost a key battle when Weeks ruled that the statement would remain in evidence.

Demery and Green were charged in August 1993 after a body found in a South Carolina swamp was identified as the elder Jordan.

Green's trial has not yet been scheduled.

Special Championship
June 17, 1996
By Chris Sheridan

His body shook as he sobbed uncontrollably. He hugged the basketball as tight as he wished he could hold his father.

In his hour of triumph, as the Chicago Bulls won the NBA championship on Father's Day, Michael Jordan grieved with a display of raw, touching emotion that brought closure to the personal hell endured so publicly by the greatest basketball player in the world.

"I can't even put it into words," said Jordan, whose crying spasm on the floor of the lockerroom was broadcast to an audience that had tuned in to see the crowning moment in his team's season of unprecedented accomplishments. Viewers saw that, then watched the unexpected,

"I knew he was watching. This was for dad. I'm very happy for him, Jordan said. "I never doubted that I could get back this moment, and the fact that it happened on Father's Day makes it even more special.

Chicago Bulls' Michael Jordan ponders a question after practice, June 3, 1996. (AP Photo/Charles Bennett)

The last time Jordan won a title was in June 1993, and his father was a public presence back then, speaking publicly on his son's behalf because Jordan was irked at the media for chronicling his gambling exploits in the newspapers and on television.

Two months later, his father James was dead, killed by Larry Martin Demery and Daniel Andre Green while napping alongside the road late one night in the sleek, red Lexus his son had bought for him.

"He made a statement like, `What is this?' or `What's going on?' As soon as these words were out of his mouth, Daniel cut him off. By that I mean he shot him. Daniel just shot him," Demery testified. "We both stood there and watched the man die."

The two realized who they had killed when they rifled through his possessions. After stealing an NBA championship ring off James Jordan's finger, stealing his shoes and his clothes, Demery and Green dumped the body in a swamp in South Carolina, then went joyriding in the car, all the while making phone calls from the dead man's cellular phone.

The telephone calls helped investigators track the two men down, and both were found guilty of murder and sentenced to life in prison.

Michael Jordan was exposed to all the horrible public details of his father's death, and even as the years moved on, Jordan remained uncomfortable discussing the subject.

That's what made Sunday night's display of emotion all the more gripping, a man who lost his father grieving publicly on Father's Day during a moment of joy he strived so hard to recapture.

"This is probably the hardest time for me to play the game of basketball," Jordan said. "I had a lot of things on my heart, on my mind. I had a lot to think about, and maybe my mind wasn't geared to where it was.

"But I think deep down inside it was geared to what was important to me, which was my family and my father not being here to see this. It was a tough time for me."

5

Three More Rings

Old Teammates
June 4, 1996
By Rick Gano

Former North Carolina players, from left, Sam Perkins, James Worthy and Michael Jordan talk during halftime of a college basketball game against Wake Forest in Chapel Hill, N.C., February 10, 2007. (AP Photo/ Gerry Broome)

They won a national championship together at North Carolina. Now for the second time in the 1990s, Michael Jordan and Sam Perkins are on opposite sides in the NBA Finals.

Perkins and Jordan were teammates as Tar Heels in 1982 when North Carolina claimed its first national title on a late Jordan jumper that beat Georgetown.

Jordan has since added two gold medals and three NBA titles. Perkins was also on the 1984 Olympic team that won the gold, but he's still searching for his NBA title.

"He was a real good player in college. When he went to the NBA, he just left me in the cellar. I mean, the man just took off," Perkins said of Jordan.

Perkins was with the Lakers in 1991 and hit a game-winning shot in the opener before the Bulls won the next four games for their first of three straight crowns. Now Jordan is blocking Perkins' path again.

"I'm happy for Sam. I'm here to deprive him of what he's hoping to attain. I've always respected him," Jordan said.

"We have a similar background. I'm all for North Carolina, except for this circumstance. It's going to be good to see George Karl and Sam, but I don't have a problem beating them."

Karl, the Sonics' coach, also played under Dean Smith at Carolina.

———

GLOBAL SWARMING: Six hundred million households will be able to watch the NBA Finals on TV. The league has agreements with 80 broadcasters, reaching 169 countries. About 1,400 media credentials have been issued, including 200 to international media members from 34 countries.

———

CBA ROOTS: Chicago's Phil Jackson and Seattle's George Karl each coached five seasons in the Continental Basketball Association.

Jackson posted a 117-90 record with the Albany Patroons and Karl was 176-66 with the Patroons and the Montana Golden Nuggets.

Jackson is the only coach to win a title in both the CBA and NBA. He led the Patroons to the 1984 title and the Bulls to championships in 1991, 1992 and 1993.

Karl led Albany to the best record in CBA history at 50-6 in 1990-91 and his top player that season was Vincent Askew, now a reserve with the Sonics and a two-time MVP in the CBA.

Jackson is the most successful playoff coach in the NBA history, taking a a 77-29 record (.726) into Wednesday night's Game 1. Karl is 33-33.

———

FINALS FORMAT: This is the 12th straight year and 16th overall the Finals has used a 2-3-2 scheduling format instead of 2-2-1-1-1.

"A 2-3-2 series is very difficult" for the team with four home games, said Bulls coach Phil Jackson. "If you can come in and get one game on the road and then you have three home games in a row, you feel great about going back and having a chance to close it out on your homecourt. It's really a psychological advantage."

But, historically, teams with the four home games like Jackson's have the real advantage.

Only three times since 1985 has the team with three middle games at home won the series, including the Bulls in 1993 when they beat Phoenix.

―――

SCORING CHAMPS: The Bulls are trying to become the first team since the 1975 Golden State Warriors to lead the league in scoring and win the NBA title. They would be just the ninth team overall to do so. Chicago averaged 105.2 points per game this season.

―――

WANNA BET?: The winner's going to be stuffed. Chicago Mayor Richard M. Daley and his counterpart, Seattle's Norm Rice, are making a tasty best on the NBA Finals.

If the Sonics win, Daley will send Rice some of Chicago's finest fare _ pizza, beef sandwiches, ribs, cheesecake, hot dogs and Mexican food.
If the Bulls win, Rice will ship salmon, sweet onions, cheese, oysters, fried chicken, wine from his region and coffee.

―――

ROYAL TREATMENT: Princess Diana will be in Chicago for three days this week to help raise funds for breast cancer research. His Airness, Michael Jordan, hopes Her Highness will be given the proper respect and treatment.

"I hope she gets as much privacy as she can get. With you guys here, she won't get that much," Jordan told reporters this week.

"For a person who's been in that spotlight pretty often, I like to get as much privacy as possible and enjoy the city. I hope she gets a chance to do that. I know she's admired by many people here in the States and hopefully they can give her the space to relax."

Anticipation
June 11, 1996
By Mike Nadel

Chicago Bulls' Michael Jordan comes down on top of Seattle SuperSonics' David Wingate in the second quarter, June 7, 1996. (AP Photo/Michael Conroy)

George Karl has Worm on the brain. Shawn Kemp already is talking about "losing like a man." Gary Payton speaks of lessons learned for future seasons.

Beaten physically and mentally by the Chicago Bulls, the Seattle SuperSonics sound like a team ready to mail in Game 4 of the NBA Finals.

"There's nothing wrong with losing ... to a better team," Kemp said Monday, the day after the Bulls took a 3-0 series lead with a decisive victory at Key Arena. "If we're going to end it, we've just got to end it in a manly way."

Apparently, they won't be borrowing any of Dennis Rodman's feather boas or mascara for Wednesday night, when Chicago can complete the sweep _ and the best season in NBA history.

Karl continues to complain about Rodman's ability to "create a circus and get away with it," referring more to the Worm's cunning and sometimes dirty on-court tricks than the flamboyant forward's outrageous appearance.

"With his elbowing, his grabbing, his walking underneath players," the Seattle coach said, "is he winning with that or is he hurting the game with that?"

In dealing with the media, Karl kept bringing up Rodman even when asked questions about other subjects.

For example, queried about the Bulls' strengths, Karl said: "They're an obnoxiously good rebounding team, led by Dennis Rodman, who is obnoxious."

It's a sign that Rodman, and the Bulls, already have won.

And don't think the Worm doesn't know it.

"The whole game (Sunday), they were so concentrating on what I was doing, saying and how I was acting on the floor that they forgot how to play basketball," Rodman said. "When you try to lure some animal into the burrow and all of a sudden he takes the bait, he's got a problem.

"After that, the game was over."

Michael Jordan is eagerly anticipating the series being over.

Jordan, who had 36 points in Game 3, is closing in on his goal of securing a title for those without rings _ teammates such as Luc Longley, Ron Harper, Steve Kerr and Toni Kukoc. Jordan and Scottie Pippen are the only players remaining from Chicago's championship teams of 1991, 1992 and 1993.

"So many people have never experienced winning," Jordan said. "It's been my motivation all season to help them. I've said, `Hang on to my coattails, and I'm going to take you where you need to go.'

"You can see signs of their appetite growing, being so close right now. They get up every day with a sparkle in their eyes. I'm pretty sure that when we win this thing, you're going to see them crying like babies."

Few will forget the way Jordan hugged the championship trophy, tears rolling down his cheeks, after carrying the Bulls to their first title back in '91.

Having leaders like Jordan and Pippen, as well as Rodman, John Salley and James Edwards, current Bulls who won titles with Detroit, is comforting to other Chicago players.

"When guys have been there before, you know they can get there again," Longley said.

"Michael promised me a championship ring," Harper said. "And he's getting ready to deliver."

It's not surprising that the Bulls are full of anticipation. After all, they've been thinking about this for months. They won an NBA-record 72 regular-season games. And a victory Wednesday would give them the best postseason mark ever, 15-1.

"I don't think it's been that easy," Jordan said. "Everything's been painted as a golden stream to a championship, but dealing with expectations is sometimes hard. It's dangerous, because you can fall prey to that and forget about playing the game and doing your job. But we've done our job all year long ... and this is the reward."

For Seattle, the feeling is more resignation than anticipation.

"They've been here three times and won it three times. We're just our first time being here," Payton said. "This is a learning experience to me. They're teaching us a lesson."

When not ranting about Rodman, Karl kept repeating that "the Bulls are beatable," as if tying to convince himself.

Technically, of course, he's right.

But even he knows that his Sonics have little chance of winning four straight against a Chicago team that is 86-11 since November. So he's not sure what he'll tell his club before Wednesday's game.

Chicago Bulls guard Michael Jordan flies to the hoop past Seattle SuperSonics defenders during Game 3 in the NBA Finals, in Seattle. The Bulls beat the Sonics 108-86 to take a 3-0 lead in the best-of-seven series, June 9, 1996, (AP Photo/Beth A. Keiser)

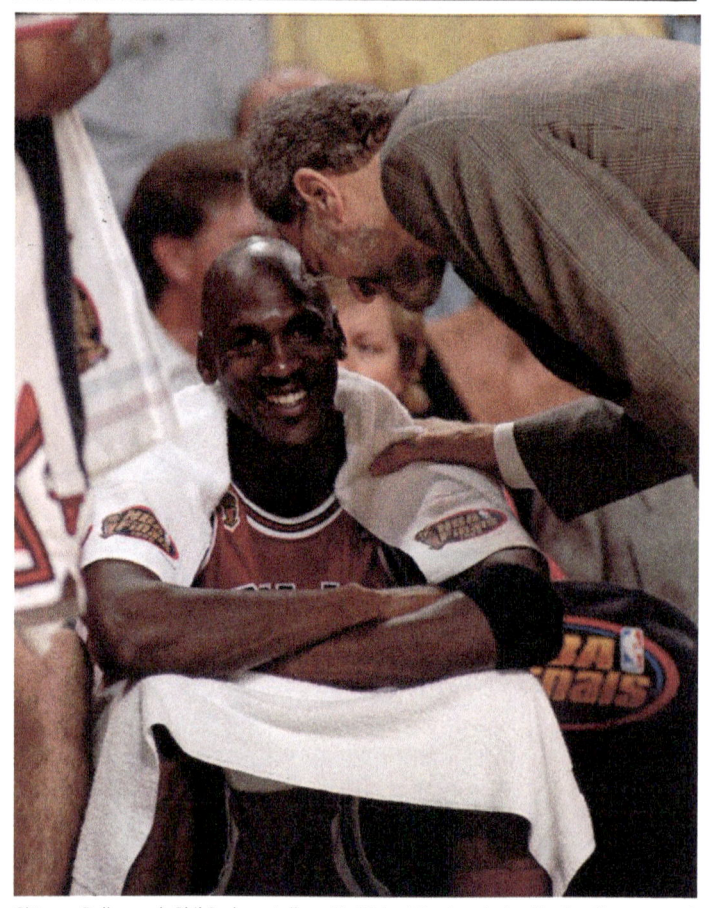

Chicago Bulls coach Phil Jackson talks with Michael Jordan during the fourth quarter of Game 4 in the NBA Finals in Seattle. The Seattle SuperSonics beat the Bulls 107-86, but the Bulls still lead the series 3-1, June 12, 1996, (AP Photo/Beth A. Keiser)

"I had my Knute Rockne speech (Sunday) and it didn't work very well. There's got to be a Part II," Karl said. "I just want my team to play like they have all year."

All year, that is, until they ran into the Bulls.

Special Meaning Behind Title
June 17, 1996
By Chris Sheridan

Chicago Bulls guard Michael Jordan slams one home against the Seattle SuperSonics during the first quarter of Game 5 in the NBA Finals, in Seattle, June 14, 1996 (AP Photo/Bob Galbraith)

His body shook as he sobbed uncontrollably. He hugged the basketball as tight as he wished he could hold his father.

In his hour of triumph, as the Chicago Bulls won the NBA championship on Father's Day, Michael Jordan grieved with a display of raw, touching emotion that brought closure to the personal hell endured so publicly by the greatest basketball player in the world.

"I can't even put it into words," said Jordan, whose crying spasm on the floor of the lockerroom was broadcast to an audience that had tuned in to see the crowning moment in his team's season of unprecedented accomplishments. Viewers saw that, then watched the unexpected,

"I knew he was watching. This was for dad. I'm very happy for him, Jordan said. "I never doubted that I could get back this moment, and the fact that it happened on Father's Day makes it even more special.

The last time Jordan won a title was in June 1993, and his father was a public presence back then, speaking publicly on his son's behalf because Jordan was irked at the media for chronicling his gambling exploits in the newspapers and on television.

Two months later, his father James was dead, killed by Larry Martin Demery and Daniel Andre Green while napping alongside the road late one night in the sleek, red Lexus his son had bought for him.

"He made a statement like, `What is this?' or `What's going on?' As soon as these words were out of his mouth, Daniel cut him off. By that I mean he shot him. Daniel just shot him," Demery testified. "We both stood there and watched the man die."

The two realized who they had killed when they rifled through his possessions. After stealing an NBA championship ring off James Jordan's finger, stealing his shoes and his clothes, Demery and Green dumped the body in a swamp in South Carolina, then went joyriding in the car, all the while making phone calls from the dead man's cellular phone.

The telephone calls helped investigators track the two men down, and both were found guilty of murder and sentenced to life in prison.

Michael Jordan was exposed to all the horrible public details of his father's death, and even as the years moved on, Jordan remained uncomfortable discussing the subject.

That's what made Sunday night's display of emotion all the more gripping, a man who lost his father grieving publicly on Father's Day during a moment of joy he strived so hard to recapture.

"This is probably the hardest time for me to play the game of basketball," Jordan said. "I had a lot of things on my heart, on my mind. I had a lot to think about, and maybe my mind wasn't geared to where it was.

"But I think deep down inside it was geared to what was important to me, which was my family and my father not being here to see this. It was a tough time for me."

Michael Jordan, left, and Scottie Pippen of the Chicago Bulls celebrate with champagne in the locker room after they defeated the Seattle SuperSonics , 87-75, in Game 6 to win the NBA Championship in Chicago, June 16, 1996. (AP Photo/Beth A. Keiser)

Another Ring
June 14, 1997
By Chris Sheridan

With Michael Jordan carrying the load, the Chicago Bulls captured their fifth professional basketball championship in seven years Friday night with a thrilling 90-86 victory over the Utah Jazz.

The Bulls wrapped up the best-of-seven series 4-2 on a clutch shot not by Jordan, but by fellow guard Steve Kerr. It ended what had easily been the most competitive of the Bulls' title series.

Jordan finished with 39 points in the final game, two days after scoring 38 in a Bulls win as he played with a stomach virus. He was named the most valuable player of the National Basketball Association finals, an award he has won each year the Bulls captured the title (1991-93, 1996-97).

"Who else can it be? Five titles, five MVPs," NBA commissioner David Stern said. "He showed us he's the best basketball player in the world."

The game hung in the balance until the final seconds against the Jazz, a dogged opponent who made crucial mistakes that cost them a chance to become the first team to take the Bulls to a seventh game in the finals.

It was Jordan who set up Kerr's basket with seven seconds left and the scored tied at 86-86. Jordan drew two players to him before passing the ball to Kerr, who calmly made the shot from 18 feet away.

The Jazz lost the ball as they tried to tie and Chicago added a final basket. It was a crushing ending for Jazz veterans John Stockton and Karl Malone, who had edged Jordan for the regular-season MVP award.

Since 1991, the only two years the Bulls didn't win the title were 1994, when Jordan was playing baseball, and 1995, when Jordan had just come out of retirement.

New Rivals
June 16, 1997

The Chicago Bulls' Michael Jordan (23) goes up and under Utah Jazz forward Karl Malone, left, as he drives to the hoop during the third quarter of Game 2 in the NBA Finals, June 4, 1997. (AP Photo/Beth A. Keiser)

The Chicago Bulls' Michael Jordan (23) tries to work his way around Utah Jazz guard John Stockton during the first quarter of Game 3 of the NBA Finals, June 6, 1997. (AP Photo/Susan Ragan)

A dejected Chicago Bulls' Michael Jordan heads off the court following the Bulls' 78-73 loss to the Utah Jazz in Game 4 of the NBA Finals, June 8, 1997. (AP Photo/ Douglas C. Pizac)

The Chicago Bulls' Michael Jordan celebrates after the Bulls beat the Utah Jazz 90-86 in Game 6 to win the NBA championship, June 13, 1997. (AP Photo/Morry Gash)

Flu Game Shatters Rating
June 17, 1997
By David Bauder

Chicago Bulls Scottie Pippen, right, embraces an exhausted Michael Jordan following their 90-88 win in Game 5 of the NBA Finals against the Utah Jazz, in Salt Lake City. An auction company says Jordan's shoes from the famous flu game of the 1997 NBA finals have sold for more than $100,000. The shoes were owned by a Utah Jazz ball boy who befriended Jordan when the Chicago Bulls visited Salt Lake City, June 11, 1997. (AP Photo/Jack Smith, File)

Proving his mettle on the court and on the tube, Michael Jordan helped NBC score another lopsided win in the Nielsen Media Research ratings by leading the Chicago Bulls to their fifth championship.

The week's most watched program was Game 5 of the National Basketball Association's Finals, in which Jordan shook off the flu to nail the game-winning shot against the Utah Jazz.

The Bulls' title-clinching win in Game 6 was No. 2 in the week's ratings.

NBC needed no last-minute shots to dominate the competition with a 9.4 rating and 18 share. CBS was second with a 7.1 rating and 14 share, followed by ABC's 6.3 rating and 12 share, and Fox's 4.5 rating and 9 share.

Fox, which has made a point of trying to run a handful of new shows in the summer, was the only one of the top four networks to improve its ratings over the same week in 1996.

The 1997 NBA Finals finished as the second-highest rated championship series ever, behind only the 1993 Bulls-Phoenix Suns series. Last year's Bulls-Seattle SuperSonics series falls to No. 3.

All of those series had Jordan in common.

NBC estimates that last week's fifth game had the most viewers of any NBA Finals game, with the sixth game on Friday night having the third most viewers. The deciding game of the 1993 series had the second most viewers.

Kobe Bryant of the Los Angeles Lakers goes in for a layup against the Utah Jazz during the second half of their playoff game, May 8, 1997. (AP Photo/Chris Pizzello)

Heir Apparent
December 18, 1997
By Miks Nadel

"The next Michael Jordan."

How many times has the original heard that over the last dozen years?

"A couple," Jordan said. "But I think that's a beautiful part of the game. If you didn't have this, it would be hype-less."

And nobody could accuse Wednesday's game between Jordan's Chicago Bulls and Kobe Bryant's Los Angeles Lakers of being without hype.

It was the old geezers vs. the young whippersnappers, the two-time defending NBA champions against the supposed team of tomorrow. Mostly, though, it was the soon-to-be-35 Jordan vs. the 19-year-old Bryant _ the latest in a long line of next Michael Jordans.

As usual, Air Jordan got the better of Heir Jordan.

"Michael loves this stuff," teammate Ron Harper said after Jordan's 36 points led the Bulls to a 104-83 victory. "(Bryant) is a very young player who someday may take his throne, but I don't think Michael's ready to give up his throne yet.

"He came out to show everybody that he's Air Jordan still."

Bryant did fine, too.

His career-high 33-point night included several highlight-film-worthy moves reminiscent of, well, a certain bald-headed, tongue-wagging country-kid-turned-big-city-CEO.

"I had that same type of vibrancy when I was young," said Jordan, who is gunning for his 10th NBA scoring title. "It's exciting to match wits against physical skills, knowing that I've been around the game long enough that if I have to guard a Kobe Bryant ... I can still hold my own."

He can still hold his own.

For a spell during the second half, he and Bryant played "anything you can do, I can do better." They exchanged jumpers and driving layups, and kept the game interesting even though the Bulls never led by fewer than 16 points after halftime.

"It's very tough for me not to get into a one-on-one confrontation, especially when he scores on me," Jordan said. "It's a natural tendency, as a competitor, to show you can score on him. It takes a lot of discipline to not get caught up in that and think team first."

The game being so one-sided made it easier for both Jordan and Bryant to justify their one-upmanship.

"It's definitely a lot of fun playing against Michael," Bryant said. "I just accept challenges. I want to guard Mike. If he goes around you, he goes around you."

Bryant really put on a show after Jordan left midway through the fourth quarter, scoring 12 of his points _ including a rim-shaking windmill dunk. Jordan said Bryant's potential is limitless.

"The biggest challenge that he has is utilizing what he's got, to improve on it each and every day," Jordan said. "That's tough. That's experience. That's the thing that Larry Bird and Magic Johnson taught me.

"There's no doubt that he has the skills to take over a game. Somehow he has to pass it on to the team and do it at times where it doesn't take away from what the team's trying to do."

It took Jordan years to learn how to do that, and sometimes he still fails. "It's all a learning process," Jordan said.

In the spirit of education, Bryant approached Jordan during Wednesday's fourth quarter.

"He asked me about my post move ... which kind of shocked me," Jordan said. "I felt like an old man."

He sure didn't look like a geezer. He looked every bit like the one and only, not an imitation or wannabe.

"When a guy asks me for advice in the middle of a game, a young player such as him, that's the only time I really feel old," Jordan said. "Physically, I feel great."

Chicago Bulls Michael Jordan (23) reaches to defend against Los Angeles Lakers Kobe Bryant (8) during the second quarter action in Inglewood, California. Lakers routed the Bulls, 112-87, February 1, 1998. (AP Photo/Kevork Djansezian)

Final Dance 98
June 1, 1998
By Nancy Armour

Chicago Bulls' Michael Jordan, right, holds his fifth Most Valuable Player award with Bill Russell of the Boston Celtics at a ceremony. Jordan previously won the award in 1998, 1991, 1992, and 1996. Russell, who presented the award, is the only other five-time winner, May 18, 1998. (AP Photo/Jay Crihfield)

Michael Jordan has five NBA Finals MVP awards and, in what could be his last season, is a favorite for a sixth. Yet Scottie Pippen's defense is a big part of why the Chicago Bulls are closing in on another title.

So who gets the MVP? His Airness? Or his longtime Heir Apparent?

"From my situation, it's hard to merit who would be (MVP)," coach Phil Jackson said. "And I really don't like to think about it until we're finished, but I would say that between Michael and Scottie, you've got a real tough choice."

Of course, the Bulls have to win the NBA title before anyone starts handing out awards. With a 3-1 lead over the Utah Jazz, they could do that as early as tonight.

But if Chicago does win, the choice for MVP won't be an easy one. On the one hand, there's Jordan, simply the greatest player of his era and possibly of all time. At 35, he lacks some of the speed and flash of his younger days, but he makes up for it with improved finesse and skill.

He won his fifth regular-season MVP award this year, and has led the Bulls in scoring in each of their 19 playoff games. He's hit game-winning shots and made acrobatic dunks and driving layups that the average human couldn't match. He scored 34 points against the Jazz on Wednesday and barely broke a sweat.

Most importantly, he's the soul of the Bulls team, inspiring his teammates, yelling at them when they make mistakes, even chastising the referees when he feels they've made a bad call.

"He's the greatest closer ever," teammate Jud Buechler said. "He's the most competitive person I've ever been around."

But on the other hand, there's Pippen, who's finally stepped out of Jordan's shadow during the playoffs. Without his superb defense, the Bulls might not have made it past Indiana in the Eastern Conference finals, and they likely wouldn't have a 3-1 lead over the Jazz.

"I saw Classic Sports, the championship Suns vs. Bulls in 1993, and I was looking at the difference between Michael and Scottie in five years. How athletic they were at one time," Jackson said. "They are still great athletes, but how much has been diminished by injuries and age.

"Scottie is still so terrific in his speed and anticipation. He's always there, he's always a harassing person."

The Jazz can vouch for that. Utah entered the series as the league's top shooting team, thanks to their famed pick-and-roll offense. But Pippen has helped squeeze the pick-and-roll and close off Utah's other favorite option, a driving Karl Malone.

He's been floating all over the floor, prowling the top of the key one second, moving to double Malone the next. He's been so bothersome that Utah complains he's got to be playing illegal defense, but Pippen makes sure he's never in one place long enough to get caught.

"I use my speed, my quickness, my size to roam around the court and stay aggressive on the ball," he said. "To the Utah Jazz, I'm probably the most illegal guy that's ever played a game.

"But I'm being aggressive, and the officials see me as being the aggressor," he said. "I'm trying to stay active and doing a good job of pretty much recovering to my man or getting to the basket to get the defensive rebound, whatever it takes."

His game hasn't just been defense, though. In Game 4, he scored 28 points _ including five 3-pointers _ and dished out five assists to go with his nine rebounds.

So, the MVP award goes to...

"Both," teammate Steve Kerr said, smiling. "Co-MVPs."

Jordan's Future
June 3, 1998
By Rick Gano

Michael Jordan has said it before. Many times. And now he's said it again at the NBA Finals. He doesn't know what he'll be doing next season.

Could be golf. Could be hoops. Maybe running his own business empire.

He did claim Tuesday that how the Chicago Bulls do in the finals against the Utah Jazz won't affect his plans.

"At the end of the season, it's about evaluating where the organization is and some of the decisions they have to go through and base my decision on that," Jordan said.

"I've lost at the end of the season before and continued to play and won at the end of the season and continued to play.

"If my hunger and my excitement for the game still continue and I have the appetite for that at the end of the season _ win, lose or draw _ I will continue to play."

For most of the season, Jordan has attached his basketball future to the return of Coach Phil Jackson, who has openly said he is not coming back.

The Bulls' farewell saga has been replayed at every stop during the season and Scottie Pippen has even worn a "Last Dance 98" hat, a phrase used by Jackson to describe the team's final season together.

Bulls chairman Jerry Reinsdorf said last month he would be inclined to bring back all the team's major players should the Bulls win their sixth championship and that he would give Jordan ample time to make up his mind.

Chicago Bulls' Michael Jordan rests on the bench during the third quarter against the Vancouver Grizzlies in Chicago. Jordan said he definitely wants to play next season, but he still wants Coach Phil Jackson back, as well. "I mean under certain circumstances," he said at a shoot around before the Bulls' game against Vancouver. "If I don't feel it's something I'm happy with, I certainly have alternatives," March 20, 1998. (AP Photo/Michael S. Green)

Jordan hedged on his future late in the season, allowing for the possibility he could still play, even if Jackson isn't around.

Many find it hard to believe that the 35-year-old Jordan's competitive nature would allow him to leave after a loss. He's always said he wants to leave on top.

"I've had enough success to know you can't win every time at the end of the season," Jordan said. "It doesn't stick with me or drive me nuts or keep me from sleeping. That's part of the game and I can deal with losing.

"I just don't want to lose. I can deal with it, but I don't want to."

Toughest Title
June 14, 1998
By Jim Litke

This was not a movie.

He got game.

Back spasms took away his running mate. Utah's resolve scared off the rest of his help. Age took the spring from his 35-year-old legs. Fatigue did its best to take away everything else. None of that mattered.

He got game.

"I think of all the championships we won," Michael Jordan said Sunday night, "this is the toughest."

For him, no doubt it was.

He scored the last basket, the last eight points of the game, 16 of the Chicago Bulls' final 26, 45 of their total of 82. He stole the ball from Karl Malone to set up his last shot, then nearly broke Bryon Russell's ankles with a crossover dribble to open up enough space just to launch it. He watched it fall, then lowered his eyes, and with a professional's cold glare, simply turned around and headed back up the court to make one more stand.

What no one knew in those moments afterward, when he was through hugging his teammates, his opponents, his mother and the NBA's championship trophy for the sixth time, was whether this was also his last stand.

"I think everybody knows how he should be remembered," Jazz coach Jerry Sloan said. "As the greatest player that ever played."

**Career Snapshot
Number Six**

Michael Jordan 125

1998

Utah Jazz's Greg Ostertag (00) goes for a rebound against the Chicago Bulls' defense as Michael Jordan watches from the background during overtime in Game 1 of the NBA Finals in Salt Lake City, June 3, 1998. (AP Photo/Mark J. Terrill)

126   AP Editions

Chicago Bulls' Michael Jordan pulls the ball out of reach of Utah Jazz guard Jeff Hornacek, right, during third quarter action in Game 2 of the NBA Finals in Salt Lake City, June 5, 1998. (AP Photo/Mark J. Terrill)

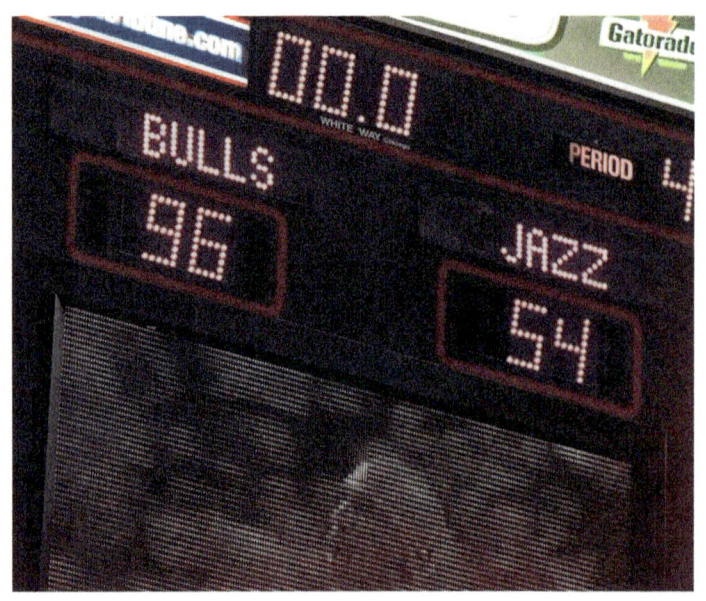

The image of Chicago Bulls' Michael Jordan is shown below the final score of Game 3 of the NBA Finals against the Utah Jazz, June 7, 1998. (AP Photo/Beth A. Keiser)

Chicago Bulls' Michael Jordan reaches high above teammates Dennis Rodman, left, Scottie Pippen, and Scott Burrell (24) for a rebound against the Utah Jazz in the second half of Game 4 in the NBA Finals, June 10, 1998. (AP Photo/Michael S. Green)

Chicago Bulls guard Michael Jordan holds up six fingers for the six NBA Championships the Bulls have won after Chicago defeated 87-86 in Salt Lake City, June 14, 1998. (AP Photo/Mark J. Terrill)

6

One Last Run

Calling it Quits
January 13, 1999
By Rick Gano

Michael Jordan's first retirement didn't last. His second, more than five years later, just might.

"It's totally different circumstances. He's a different age, he's won six titles instead of three," said guard Steve Kerr, Jordan's Chicago Bulls teammate and now a free agent.

Last time, as Jordan grieved for his murdered father, he said he'd had enough of the NBA grind, needed more time with his family and new challenges. But on that stunning October day in 1993, a 30-year-old Jordan didn't rule out a return to basketball.

After a short-lived baseball career, he came back. Did he ever, adding three more NBA titles and re-establishing himself as the game's greatest player.

Now he's ready to retire again. And as he turns 36 next month, this time, it will probably be for good. The Bulls called a news conference at the United Center, the building where Jordan held a glitzy retirement party in November 1994, the building where he so often led the team to victory.

Now it's the place where, according to a league source, Jordan planned to announce his retirement after 13 seasons with the Bulls.

"If we could have things our way, I'm sure that Michael probably could play another couple of years and would embrace the opportunity," teammate Scottie Pippen told WLS-TV this morning.

"But with a lot of the things going on in the organization, and unhappiness and things of that nature, he felt that right now, he's on top, this is the best time for him to get out," he said.

"I'm not going to get into my soliloquy about Michael Jordan until I hear it's official," Kerr said Tuesday after working on his jump shot at the Berto Center in suburban Deerfield.

Michael Jordan announces his retirement from the Chicago Bulls and the NBA during a press conference in Chicago's United Center, January 13, 1999. (AP Photo/Beth A. Keiser)

"I'm not going to be the fool who talks about it before it all happens."

Around the league and throughout the city that worships him, Jordan's impending retirement didn't come as a surprise.

But most acknowledged that neither the Bulls nor the NBA would be the same without him, especially during this lockout-shortened season.

"Losers! Losers! Losers!" 32-year-old Derrick Watt said as he left Jordan's downtown restaurant on another cold winter's day. "Without Michael, they'll be in the basement of their division."

Jordan met with a few teammates at his home Monday and told them the thought of playing an abbreviated, 50-game season wasn't enough of a challenge, the Chicago Tribune reported.

Kerr and free-agent center Luc Longley said Tuesday they hadn't heard from Jordan or the team about the retirement, and that's why they wanted to get their information directly from the source.

"He told us after the season that he didn't want to come back. But at that point, I don't know if any of us wanted to come back," Kerr said.

"We were kind of tired. But after a summer of rest _ a summer and a fall and a winter of rest _ it's easy to be rejuvenated, so everybody knew he had that option to come back. "

But now Jordan can go out as he always wanted _ on top. His last-second shot _ the last one he might ever take _ beat Utah in Game 6 last June and gave the Bulls their sixth title.

"There's a way to go out as an athlete, and that's the way to go out," said B.J. Armstrong, one of about a dozen players working out Tuesday at the Berto Center.

Armstrong, who now plays with Charlotte, is a good friend of Jordan's and a teammate on Chicago's first three NBA championship teams.

"He went out on top, he made the last shot, he made all the right plays. He's had a fabulous career and everything you could ever ask as an athlete, he's done. He had a chance to leave and this was the chance," Armstrong said.

"He's doing it his way. There's a part of me that is sad, but a part of me that is happy to see him go out on top."

He would also be going out as a five-time league MVP, 10-time league scoring champion and the No. 1 per-game scorer in NBA history.

General manager Jerry Krause, who openly feuded with Jordan, had no comment as he pulled his car into the snowy parking lot at the practice center.

Coach-in-waiting Tim Floyd wasn't saying much, either. He rolled his car window down and said: "I don't think it would be appropriate for me to say anything at this point."

In case everyone has forgotten, for a long time Jordan loudly proclaimed he had no intention of playing for any coach but Phil Jackson, who left the team after June's championship and has declined several invitations to return.

Jordan's Dream Team teammate and TV commercial sidekick Larry Bird, who retired and then returned as coach of the Indiana Pacers, jokingly suggested the NBA hadn't seen the last of His Airness:

"There comes a time in every player's career that they have to make that decision, and he feels it's his time. We want to wish he and his family well and we look forward to seeing him sometime in late March when he makes his return again in Market Square Arena."

That's where Jordan made his comeback nearly four years ago.

Johnny Bach, an assistant coach on three of the Bulls' championship teams, praised Jordan for not only his skill, but for the joy he brought to the game.

"He never looked like he'd been sentenced by a judge to play basketball," Bach said. "I've seen too many athletes not go out at the right time. They stay and struggle and lose some of the dignity they are entitled to."

Appalachian State coach Buzz Peterson called his former North Carolina roommate and put the question to him directly.

"What's going on? I've got 25 pink slip phone messages here in front of me," Peterson said. "He just laughed and said everything's coming out now and everything's being said."

Peterson said the Bulls' coaching change didn't have anything to do with Jordan's decision, but family considerations did.

"He's just run out of things to prove and he loves those kids. Whenever I talk to him, he just can't stop talking about Marcus and Jeffrey and Jasmine," Peterson said.

"Marcus and Jeffrey are playing basketball now and he could tell you how many points they scored and how many assists they had and what the final score was of every one of their games."

Never Say Never
February 15, 1999
By Jim Litke

Former NBA and Chicago Bulls superstar Michael Jordan walks off the court with his former teammate, Houston Rockets' Scottie Pippen, after the Rockets' lost to the Los Angeles Lakers, 106-90, at the Great Western Forum in Inglewood, Calif., February 28, 1999. (AP Photo/Kevork Djansezian)

He made the game up on the fly.

The best ones always do.

Michael Jordan took off plenty of times thinking one thing and wound up doing something else in the air. So what was he thinking showing up at Bulls practice Wednesday for a very public little one-on-one with Corey Benjamin?

"Today was just to break a sweat and see some of the guys and try to help the morale a little," Jordan said. "Please, don't take it any further than that."

Fine—if he returns his profile to the "low" setting. But if Jordan turns up at other NBA camps, if rumors of secret workouts and meetings abound, remember: We've seen this before.

There may be no master plan, yet, no interest in hearing what commissioner David Stern or NBC Sports boss Dick Ebersol are thinking. But if that changes, here is a graceful way for Jordan to ease back into the business: As player-coach of the Chicago Bulls; better yet, as player-assistant coach.

Something is up, and maybe it's nothing more than Jordan's basketball jones. But before he made it to Bulls' practice, he caught their sorry act in Atlanta. That's more in a week than he saw them all last season. And Monday, Jordan dropped in on old friend Patrick Ewing for a Knicks game in New York.

What no one knows—not even the man himself—is whether this little bit of competition will scratch the itch. It seems Benjamin, a reserve guard who arrived in Chicago too late for any of the six championships, has been on Jordan's "to-do" list for some time. The second-year player listed Jordan as his favorite athlete and was just plucky enough to write, offering to school the old man on what he was missing.

Calling Jordan out of retirement wasn't much different than doing it in his prime. Not if you were Corey Benjamin. People who've seen the videotape said Jordan made his first five shots, ran out to a quick 10-4 lead and coasted home 11-9.

Benjamin wasn't the only one curious whether Jordan had slipped. His old coach, Phil Jackson, the new coach in Los Angeles, and Ewing both asked in recent weeks whether he's positive he's through.

Jordan said he told them the same thing he told the New York Post last week; the tendons he severed in his right index finger 10 months ago made the question moot:

"I'm kind of glad it's not functioning perfectly," he said. "It stops me from giving any serious thought to coming back and it doesn't affect the grip on my putter one bit. My playing days are over."

With the sweat still glistening from his bout with Benjamin, Jordan didn't want to discuss the finger. "I'd rather not comment and give (the media) ammunition to talk about it."

But someone who loves being talked about couldn't stop there, either.

"You could see I can still shoot. I lost a little handle, but I can still hold my own."

Nobody at Bulls headquarters doubted that _ or seemed unsettled by the visit. Not Jerry Krause, the general manager who hastened the Bulls' breakup, nor Tim Floyd, the coach brought in to preside over the wreckage.

Asked whether he would take Jordan back, Krause had a ready answer. "I'd be a damn fool not to."

Floyd wouldn't indulge even that bit of speculation. "There's no way it's going to happen."

The lesson of Jordan's first un-retirement was never say never.

Right now the Bulls are a miserable team with one fading star _ Toni Kukoc _ two promising rookie _ Elton Brand and Ron Artest _ and $7 million in salary-cap money to spend. Out of shape as he is, Jordan makes them a contender tomorrow.

Besides, as an assistant coach, he has the cover to ease back into playing and Floyd gets to keep his job. Jordan takes the $1 million exemption as a veteran player, then gets Bulls management to pay him 10 times that for coaching. The last step is to get management to bundle Kukoc and a No. 1 draft pick in a trade.

The Lakers' Glen Rice is an immediate possibility. Add Jordan's powers of persuasion to Kukoc's salary slot and the names heading Krause's wish list _ Detroit's Grant Hill and San Antonio's Tim Duncan _ suddenly don't seem as far-fetched.

There is a precedent, even. Bill Russell was Boston's player-coach from the 1966-67 season until 1968-69. After winning the championship nine times in his first 10 years as a player, he won twice more in his last two seasons doing double-duty.

But Russell was 32, and the Celtic teams he coached were loaded. Jordan turns 37 next February and would command a bunch of hand-me-downs, leftovers and might-be-somedays.

Dickey Simpkins, one of his few pals still on the laugha-Bulls says that's one reason the chances of Jordan coming back right now are "Zero."

Yet he doesn't sound quite as final as the number he throws out.

"It could change," Simpkins said with a laugh." "By the end of the month, it could change."

You're a Wizard, Michael
January 19, 2000
By Joseph White

Former basketball player Chicago Bulls' Michael Jordan smiles as he answers questions from the media at the MCI Center in Washington. The Wizards announced that Jordan will join the Wizards as part-owner and head of basketball operations, January 19, 2000. (AP Photo/Pablo Martinez Monsivais)

His Airness is back in basketball.

Michael Jordan, who retired one year ago after leading the Chicago Bulls to a sixth NBA title, joined the struggling Washington Wizards today as part-owner.

"This is new to me ... being in a city to give my support to another team," Jordan said. "Normally, I am in support of the Chicago Bulls."

Jordan said it would "take some time" to turn around the Wizards, who are 12-27.

"Yeah, it's different," he said. "I don't get to play. I don't get to wear a Wizards' uniform, but I will have influence with the players who wear the uniform."

Mixed Reaction
January 19, 2000
By Nancy Armour

Washington Wizards head of basketball operations Michael Jordan ponders a question during a news conference at the MCI Center in Washington, June 14, 2000. (AP Photo/Hillery Smith Garrison)

Go ahead, Washington, borrow Michael Jordan. No matter what city he's in, what team he's with or what job he holds, he's always going to belong to the Windy City.

Like a parent watching a child go to college, Chicagoans greeted Jordan's announcement Wednesday that he was joining the Wizards as a part-owner with a mixture of happiness and regret.

"It's sad that he won't be a part of the Bulls. But it is great that he will be in basketball," said Lance Fithian, a commodities broker who was working out at the Gold Coast Multiplex, an upscale health club where Jordan still plays an occasional pickup game.

It was only about a year ago _ Jan. 13, 1999, to be exact _ that Jordan hung up his Bulls uniform.

Chicago fans are still coming to grips with the reality he's not coming back. He gave them six NBA championships in eight years, an excuse to party in Grant Park every June, and countless "Michael memories."

Though he grew up in North Carolina, Chicago became his home, and the city considered him an adopted son. He played pickup games on city playgrounds and watched the Cubs at Wrigley Field. When the United Center was built, a statue of Jordan went out front. It still draws dozens of fans every day.

And when Jordan retired the first time, he kept his ties to Chicago intact. When he tried pro baseball, he did it with Jerry Reinsdorf's other team, the Chicago White Sox.

"In a perfect world, Michael would have been a Bull for life," said John Paxson, Jordan's teammate for the first three titles and now a broadcaster for the Bulls.

"I'm sure there's a part of all of us that would have liked to see the organization utilize him in some way," Paxson said. "But it's not a perfect world."

While Paxson and Johnnie "Red" Kerr, Chicago's first coach, found a home with the Bulls when they retired, fans weren't surprised Jordan went elsewhere. His relationship with chairman Jerry Reinsdorf deteriorated in recent years, and no one would ever mistake him and general manager Jerry Krause for friends.

Jordan blames Reinsdorf and Krause for forcing Phil Jackson out and breaking up the Bulls, and he hasn't set foot in the United Center for a basketball game since his retirement.

"For all he's done for this team and organization, we were hoping he'd be able to come back here," said Hersey Hawkins, a Chicago native now with the Bulls. "I don't know all the ins and the outs of the situation. I think it's sad and unfortunate he's not here."

In a written statement, Reinsdorf wished Jordan well.

"Michael will forever be a special part of the Bulls family," said Reinsdorf, who was at the baseball owner's meeting in Arizona and had no other comment.

"He has always thrived on challenges and opportunities. I expect nothing less from him now," Reinsdorf said. "Personally, I wish him all the best and look forward to discussing this new challenge with him when we next speak."

While fans aren't sure what kind of front-office man Jordan will make, they also said they don't think it really matters. Jordan's name alone will draw fans to Wizards' game, and he'll give the struggling team credibility it never would have had otherwise.

The entire NBA benefits from Jordan getting back into the game, fans added. And if he's got to go somewhere else, at least he's not going as a player.

"Wherever he is wanted, that is where he should go," said Elliot Wexler, a ticket broker. "At least his statue is still out at the United Center."

Jordan Returns
September 25, 2001
By Joseph White

Washington Wizard's Michael Jordan addresses members of the media for the first time since announcing his return to the NBA. The 38-year old superstar who retired three years ago from the Chicago Bulls, said he's returning to the sport he loves, October 1, 2001 (AP Photo/Doug Mills)

Michael Jordan made his comeback official, announcing he will return to play in the NBA and sign a two-year contract with the Washington Wizards. "I am returning as a player to the game I love," Jordan said in a news release issued through his management agency that confirmed the worst-kept secret in basketball.

Not Just Another Game
January 19, 2002
By Nancy Armour

Washington Wizards Michael Jordan composes himself as the crowd at the United Center gives him a standing ovation prior the game against the Chicago Bulls, January 19, 2002. (AP Photo/Paul Sancya)

His watery eyes said it all.

No matter how many times he said this was just like any other game, his reaction to the fans' thunderous ovation Saturday afternoon said just how much coming home meant to Michael Jordan.

As United Center announcer Ray Clay introduced Jordan before his first game in Chicago as a visiting player, the sellout crowd stood and started clapping and screaming. At first, the Washington Wizards' leading scorer tried to ignore it, looking down at his blue-and-white Air Jordans and chewing on his lip.

But the ovation continued for almost 3 minutes, and Jordan finally looked up. His eyes filled with tears and he glanced around the arena that will always be home no matter whose jersey he's wearing. He gave a shaky smile and waved at the fans, who adore him for the six titles he won with the Chicago Bulls even if he's no longer wearing that familiar old red-and-black No. 23.

One fan summed it up best, carrying a sign that read, simply, "Thanks, Mike." Clearly moved, Jordan looked around, seeming almost stunned by the lovefest. And he had to have smiled when fans booed when the lights went out for the Bulls' introduction before their game against the Wizards.

The fans cheered every move Jordan made—even when he fouled Ron Artest. When he made his first basket, a 15-foot jumper over Kevin Ollie with 7:38 left in the first quarter, the fans yelled as if it was the game-winner.

"He's smart enough to know this time around, with the hand he's been dealt, he's got to keep his focus," said David Falk, Jordan's agent. "He's not worried about what's going to happen next year, he's not worried probably about what's going to happen next week.

"He's trying to get out of Chicago and a circus-like atmosphere with a victory."

And what a circus it was. When he arrived at the United Center about 2 hours before the game, it was just like old times. A media crowd was waiting for him, and with flashbulbs popping and cameras rolling, he walked down the familiar hallway. People shouted questions at him as his security people tried to shelter him from all the jostling.

He stopped to talk with Carmen Villafane, a fan who's become a friend over the last 13 years.

"He just said, `How's it going? I'll talk to you after the game,'" Villafane said.

Then Jordan moved on, heading for the locker room. And that's when it got really weird.

"Hey Michael!" someone yelled, "what's it going to feel like going to the visitor's locker room?"

"I don't even know where it is," he cracked.

Washington Wizards' Michael Jordan, left, and Chicago Bulls' Ron Artest battle for position during the fourth quarter. Jordan scored 16 points in his return to Chicago in the Wizards 77-69 win, January 19, 2002. (AP Photo/Paul Sancya)

It's been 3 1/2 years since Jordan walked away after the Bulls won their sixth NBA championship. He vowed never to play for a coach other than Phil Jackson and swore the Chicago Bulls uniform was the only one he'd wear. But there he was, in the blue-and-black of the Wizards right down to his Air Jordans. Fans have forgiven his defection, choosing instead to blame Bulls chairman Jerry Reinsdorf and general manager Jerry Krause for chasing him out of town.

Neither Reinsdorf nor Krause were there Saturday. Reinsdorf was in Arizona, and Krause was on a scouting trip.

And there was no question whose side the fans were on. It was only the second sellout this season at the United Center, and the Bulls' first network television appearance in two seasons.

Kids in Jordan jerseys—both the new and old versions—were lined up in the stands above the tunnel where teams enter well before the game. One child, wearing a Jordan Wizards jersey—held up a sign that read, "Mr. Jordan, my X-mas present was to see you play!"

"You know the competitor," said Rod Higgins, who became Jordan's best friend when he arrived in Chicago and is now the Wizards' general manager. "I don't think this game is any different in terms of how important it is to win."

The watery eyes said different.

Teary Goodbye
February 9, 2003
By Chris Sheridan

On a night for Michael Jordan, all he was missing was the game-winning shot.

Jordan said goodbye to the All-Star game with his eyes teary and his game a bit blemished as the West beat the East 155-145 in double overtime Sunday night.

A last-minute starter after Vince Carter relinquished his spot, Jordan had a poor start, a bad finish and then a good one. After clanging the potential winning shot off the iron at the end of regulation, Jordan made a high-arching 15-footer with 4.8 seconds left in overtime to give the East a two-point lead.

Kobe Bryant tied it, however, by making two foul shots with 1 second left, and Jordan's final shot of the first overtime was blocked just before the buzzer.

MVP Kevin Garnett scored nine of his 37 points in the second overtime as Jordan watched the final five minutes from the bench. It was the first double-overtime game in All-Star history.

Although Jordan missed his first seven shots, had four others rejected and blew a dunk, he did score 20 points to move past Kareem Abdul-Jabbar for most total points in All-Star history. But he needed to take 27 shots from the field, making only nine, in order to do it.

His most memorable moment came late in the first overtime, while the most poignant one came at halftime. Jordan joined singer Mariah Carey at center court, took the microphone after an extended ovation and bid a public farewell as Yao Ming, Kobe Bryant and basketball's future stood and watched. "I leave the game in good hands," Jordan said. "So many great stars rising and playing the game. I have passed on the things that Dr. J and some of the great players _ Magic Johnson, Larry Bird _ have passed on to me, I pass on to these All-Stars here, as well as to the rest of the players in the NBA.
"I want to thank you all for your support. Now I can go home and feel at peace with the game of basketball."

Washington Wizards' Michael Jordan (23), East, drives to the basket past Dallas Mavericks' Dirk Nowitzki (41), West, and Minnesota Timberwolves Kevin Garnett (21), West, during fourth quarter play of the 2003 NBA All Star Game in Atlanta, February 9, 2003. (AP Photo/Dave Martin)

- The entire evening played out as though it was a Jordan tribute.

Allen Iverson arrived at the arena wearing a retro Bulls No. 23 jersey, Yao donned a pair of powder blue low-tops, a tribute to Jordan's alma mater, North Carolina, which clashed garishly with his bright red Western Conference uniform.

Carey wore a Bulls jersey and a Wizards uniform top during a halftime show dedicated to Jordan. Several of the players wore Air Jordan shoes, and all of them stood in a pack to applaud and hug Jordan after he gave his halftime speech.

"I'm somewhat embarrassed because I got a feeling it's going to turn into the Michael Jordan show, which I don't want it to be," he said before the game.

In the end, of course, it was.

Jordan's go-ahead shot late in the first overtime was a thing of beauty, a perfectly rotating, high-floating jumper that looked true from the moment it left his fingertips.

After hitting the shot, he drifted into a row of photographers and pumped his fist, getting a chest bump from Iverson as he went to the bench.

Turmoil in Washington

Team Letting Him Down
March 10, 2003
By Joseph White

Washington Wizards' Michael Jordan (23) looks for space under the pressing defense of New York Knicks' Kurt Thomas (40) during the second half, March, 9, 2003. (AP Photo/Frank Franklin II)

Michael Jordan is upset with his teammates. Twice in three days, he's accused them of not making the extra effort to get him to the playoffs one last time.

It's an amazing accusation. Surely these guys would jump through fire to see one of the all-time greats go out on top.

Not so, thinks Jordan, who says his self-recruited Washington Wizards twentysomethings don't match the desire of a 40-year-old man when it comes to "diving for loose balls, busting his chin and doing everything he can to get his team into the playoffs."

"It's not reciprocated from the other players on the team," Jordan said after scoring an under-supported 39 points in Sunday's 97-96 loss to the New York Knicks.

The obvious question is why. Other than an occasional moment of inspiration _ such as when Larry Hughes worked double-time to recover from an injury because Jordan did the same _ why hasn't the Jordan intensity and work ethic permeated a team starving for success?

The most obvious answer lies in the awkward relationship Jordan has with the players. He's not only a superstar with a magnified presence, but also runs the team and will return to the front office next season.

As a result, he has teammates who admire and respect him, but they've never really bonded with him. Without that, there's less of an instinct to fight for him at crunch time, whether it's diving for that extra loose ball or hustling down the court to slow down a fast break.

"You can't help but look at him differently," center Brendan Haywood said Monday. "You're not playing with a regular player. This is a guy who's going to be signing checks and deciding if we're going to be here next year."

Hughes said he's been surprised by the efforts Jordan has made to be one of the guys. Jordan will sit, talk, play cards and try to make everyone comfortable, but it's still a normal locker room.

"It's definitely different," Hughes said. "It's a not situation a lot of guys have been through. There's not a set way to handle it. He's the guy on the team, so whatever he says or does basically goes. As professional guys, we roll with it. I personally look at it as a learning experience."

But "learning experience" are the last words Jordan needs to hear with just 19 regular season games left in his basketball life. He needs players who, in his words, are "going down with no bullets."

"I'm trying to do everything I can to verbalize and physically show what it takes to win," Jordan said after Sunday's loss. "It's up to them to see that and do the extra work and do the necessary things. We have too many players making the same mistakes in March as they made in October."

Washington Wizards' Michael Jordan dives for a loose ball during the fourth quarter against the New York Knicks at Madison Square Garden in New York, March 9, 2003. (AP Photo/Ed Betz)

The Wizards are in trouble. They have lost four of five and are two games behind Milwaukee for final Eastern Conference playoff spot. They have just five home games remaining and a brutal West Coast road trip still to come. The Bucks beat them Friday to win the season tiebreaker between the two teams, prompting Jordan's first swipe at his teammates.

There's also a subplot involving leading scorer Jerry Stackhouse, who complained after Sunday's game that he wasn't getting the ball enough and implied that Collins was to blame. On Monday, Stackhouse said his comments came out stronger than he intended, but his point was still the same.

"I still say that it's not all up to me," Stackhouse said. "I'd like to come out tomorrow and have 50 and we win the game, but not all that is under my control. We still have to do some things that I feel are beneficial to me getting into the flow."

The words from Jordan and Stackhouse combined with the losses to make for a quiet practice Monday. There was none of the usual joking around on the court. Some players refused to discuss Jordan's comments with reporters, while others said they felt everybody was trying hard.

Jordan did not speak to reporters at all. Collins refused to address Stackhouse's comments. The coach let Jordan's words stand on their own.

"I don't know what else I need to add to that," Collins said. "I just think his sense of urgency is greater. He's counting down the number of games he has left. I think his words are far greater than anything I could say."

The thought that the season might end in failure, coupled with the fact that he's still playing well, would seem to open the door for Jordan to return for another season. He has consistently kept that door shut, maintaining that he's 100 percent certain to hang up the uniform for good this spring.

"Are you nuts?" said Jordan, when asked Sunday if his 39 points in defeat in had him reconsidering retirement. "All it has motivated me to do is know that some of these guys may not be here next year when I go back upstairs."

Cliffhanger
April 17, 2003
By Joseph White

Even though he won't play again, Michael Jordan managed to end the season with a cliffhanger.

Will he follow his original plan and return to the Washington Wizards' front office? Will he end up in Charlotte, N.C., to run Robert Johnson's expansion franchise?

Is there still a place for him in Chicago, now that John Paxson has been hired as general manager?

Or will Jordan find something else to do?

"Let's hope we get that squared away ASAP," Wizards coach Doug Collins said. "We need to get everything in place in terms of the hierarchy, and how it's going to be, so we can start moving in the right direction."

In the coming days, Jordan will meet with Wizards owner Abe Pollin to negotiate details of his return as president of basketball operations, the title he had to give up when he returned as a player 19 months ago. Jordan then would start talks to repurchase an ownership stake from minority owner Ted Leonsis.

One thing is for certain: If Jordan stays in Washington, he has a lot of work to do.

The Wizards finished 37-45 for the second straight year despite two solid seasons from Jordan in his second comeback. There are plenty of disgruntled players in the locker room and the talent is distributed unevenly. The team essentially will be starting from scratch once more, although the salary cap squeeze from money spent on past flops finally has eased.

Jordan knows much of the responsibility is his _ he called all the front office shots while playing. But he never expected it to be easy to transform a poorly run franchise that had developed a culture of losing throughout the 1990s. Still, it has to be pointed out that Jordan's record in his 3 1/2 seasons as the top decision-maker (110-179) is actually worse than in the 3 1/2 seasons before he arrived (116-137).

Washington Wizards' Michael Jordan waves to the crowd as he walks off the court after a post-game ceremony following the Wizards' 93-79 loss to the New York Knicks at the MCI Center in Washington, D.C., April 14, 2003. (AP Photo/Nick Wass)

"I think if I had to grade myself from 'A' to a failure, I would say that I'm still right at average," Jordan said. "I don't think I've done anything, other than take some of the financial constraints off, and put together some young talent that don't really know how to apply their talents as of right now. But they are learning.

"I wouldn't even think about giving myself an 'A' or a 'B,' because we haven't achieved the playoffs. I've still got some work to do once I go back upstairs, in terms of trying to find the right mesh to build a solid, solid base."

He could very well spend the summer saying goodbye to some of his biggest acquisitions. Jerry Stackhouse, Kwame Brown, Bryon Russell and Larry Hughes have not lived up to the lofty Jordan-Collins standards for teamwork and dedication.

Late in the season, Stackhouse even began discussing how he felt the team was restricted by Jordan's presence on the court.

Collins finally fired back.

"All these guys who thought (Jordan) took away from their games, next year they're going to find out what he brought," Collins said.

Stackhouse can opt out of his contract, which would free up about $12 million in cap money. If he does not, he could be put on the trading block.

Brown has been the subject of trade talk in the past, but the Wizards did not want to give up too soon on the No. 1 overall draft pick of two seasons ago. Bad trades have been a hallmark of the Wizards in recent years, but Brown has been such a disappointment that Jordan might be willing to risk it.

Russell and Hughes began the season as starters _ and finished deep on the bench.

What is left is a hardworking group of players including Tyronn Lue, Juan Dixon, Jared Jeffries, Bobby Simmons, Etan Thomas and Christian Laettner. There is a lot of heart in that group, but not too many wins without some help. Jordan is expected to keep Collins, who on Monday blasted some of the players for showing disrespect. Jordan and Collins have generally agreed on most personnel matters.

"I'll be here as long as Michael wants me," he said.

That is, of course, if Jordan stays in Washington.

Dumped
May 8, 2003
By Joseph White

Michael Jordan leaves the MCI Center in Washington, after a meeting with team owner Abe Pollin. Jordan isn't welcome back with the Washington Wizards, who abruptly dumped him because he failed to turn them around in his 3 1/2 seasons on and off the court. Pollin made the decision after meeting with Jordan, who was the Wizards' president before coming out of retirement to play for them the past two years, May 7, 2003. (AP Photo/Gerald Herbert)

Michael Jordan isn't used to rejection, and he didn't take it well.

At an acrimonious meeting reflective of a franchise in turmoil, Jordan was shown the door Wednesday by the Washington Wizards. Jordan went in expecting to negotiate his return to the front office, but instead was told by owner Abe Pollin that he was no longer welcome after 3 1/2 unsuccessful seasons.

"Without any prior discussion with me, ownership informed me that it had unilaterally decided to change our mutual long-term understanding," Jordan said in a statement. "I am shocked by this decision, and by the callous refusal to offer me any justification for it."

Jordan hasn't been discarded by a basketball team since he was cut from the varsity as a high-school sophomore, a setback that help motivate him into becoming one of the best players ever.

As if he were intent on making history repeat itself, Jordan quickly set in motion a possible plan to prove the Wizards wrong. It didn't take long before he was on the phone with good friend Robert Johnson, owner of the new Charlotte franchise.

"He just called to say, 'Hey, I wanted to let you know what decision has been made. When you get a chance, let's talk,'" Johnson said. "We're friends. It won't take us very long to get together."

Johnson said Jordan "can play any role he wants to play" with the Charlotte team, which starts play in 2004.

Over the last decade, Pollin's Wizards have been a chronicle of losing and embarrassment, and Wednesday's ugly series of events won't help the team's reputation.

A Wizards source, speaking on condition of anonymity, told The Associated Press that Pollin's decision was based on three factors: player dissension, a franchise still faltering after years of Jordan in charge, and deteriorating relationships throughout the organization.

"While the roster of talent he has assembled here in Washington may not have succeeded to his and my expectations, I do believe Michael's desire to win and be successful is unquestioned," Pollin said in a statement.

Pollin's statement also implied that his decision was made with minority partner Ted Leonsis, saying that: "In the end, Ted and I felt that this franchise should move in a different direction."

However, another team source, speaking on condition of anonymity, said the statement was written without Leonsis' consent and that Leonsis was not aware of Pollin's decision until the meeting.

Leonsis, who dined with Jordan on Tuesday night, arrived expecting to discuss Jordan's rejoining the team, the source said. Instead, Pollin opened with a statement saying Jordan would not be welcome back and that is was not open for discussion.

During the 30-minute meeting, Pollin offered Jordan a $10 million severance payment, according to the source, but Jordan turned it down.
Leonsis had no comment.

Jordan, who led the Chicago Bulls to six NBA titles in the 1990s, was the Wizards' president from January 2000 to September 2001 before coming out of retirement to play for them the past two years. His record was just

110-179 as the top decision-maker, a role he kept even after returning as a player.

The last few months under Jordan were particularly upsetting for Pollin, an old-school owner who has shown little tolerance for in-house turmoil.

Jordan and his teammates sniped at each other as the Wizards finished a disappointing 37-45 for the second consecutive year and missed the playoffs again. Players publicly criticized coach Doug Collins, who said they were disrespectful, and recent reports in The New York Times and The Washington Post exposed a front-office rift involving people Jordan hired.

The rest of Jordan's tenure wasn't much better. He botched the firing of coach Gar Heard three years ago and later hired Leonard Hamilton, who went 19-63. As an executive, Jordan tried to run the team from his home in Chicago, leaving a rudderless team to falter on its own.

Hamstrung by the Wizards salary-cap problems, he eventually overhauled the roster and made the team his own. Jahidi White is the only pre-Jordan player left. The biggest flop? Kwame Brown has done little since being the No. 1 overall pick in the 2001 draft.

Of course, Jordan's biggest personnel move came when he returned as a player. That helped the Wizards sell out every home game the last two seasons, giving Pollin a tidy profit.

This season, Jordan loaded the roster with Jerry Stackhouse, Bryon Russell, Larry Hughes and Charles Oakley in an effort to get to the playoffs one last time, but the chemistry was bad from the start. Players found it awkward sharing the locker room with the person in charge of their contracts, and Jordan's work ethic failed to rub off.

"He's still considered the greatest player to ever play the game of basketball. I don't think anybody can take that away from him," said Detroit Pistons guard Richard Hamilton, a promising young player traded away by Jordan.

"As a team president, I'm not sure."

156　　　　　　　　　AP Editions

Dirty Politics
October 22, 2003
By Joseph White

Basketball great Michael Jordan takes a shot on the second hole at the Mellon Mario Lemieux Celebrity Invitational in Presto, Pa., June 7, 2003. (AP Photo/Gary Tramontina)

Abe Pollin knew the decision would be unpopular. Just thinking about it the night before kept the 79-year-old Washington Wizards owner from sleeping. But there was no other choice: Michael Jordan had to go.

"It was an atmosphere on edge," Abe Pollin explained in his first in-depth interview since dismissing Jordan five months ago. "It was not a healthy atmosphere to produce a happy organization or a winning team."

Jordan essentially ran the basketball side of Pollin's organization for 3 1/2 losing seasons, including the last two as a player, until the morning of May 7.

Having retired again from the court, Jordan arrived at Pollin's office that day expecting to regain the title of president of basketball operations. But discontent with Jordan and his hand-picked coach, Doug Collins, had become evident through comments from players and staff.

"I could sense the sense of unhappiness, the sense of even maybe a little dissension in the whole organization," Pollin told The Associated Press in the interview Tuesday. "I sensed that it was a bad situation."

Although he had given a speech to his employees a week earlier hinting that Jordan could be gone, Pollin said he didn't make up his mind until the night before. He even had his communications manager draft two press releases _ one announcing Jordan's departure, the other announcing that Jordan was rehired.

"I agonized over it for days and nights, thinking, 'What is it that I have to do?'" Pollin recalled. "I'm going to think very hard about these decisions and make the best decisions that I think are best for the franchise."

Given Jordan's lack of success in Washington, the actual decision to get rid of him didn't prove as unpopular as the means.

At the meeting, Pollin didn't give Jordan a chance to make a case to stay or outline any plans for the team. It ended acrimoniously after about 20 minutes, and Jordan later termed Pollin's actions as "callous."

"I had made my decision ... and that was it," Pollin said. "I felt by sticking to my decision, I would have less embarrassment for him because if I had made him lay out some of his plans that he had maybe in mind that he was going to do for the team, and then I would say, 'I'm not accepting them,' I thought I would hurt him worse. So I tried to be as gentle as I could with Michael because I have great respect for him."

Pollin also defended his decision to announce Jordan's departure by e-mail rather than face reporters.

"I don't deal with the public face," Pollin said. "I just deal with human beings."

The public backlash was severe, so much so that a few weeks later Pollin offered to refund season-ticket deposits to anyone not happy with his off-season moves.

As it turned out, Pollin had a good summer. He hired Eddie Jordan from New Jersey to replace Collins as coach, then lured Ernie Grunfeld from Milwaukee to replace Michael Jordan in the front office.

The Wizards have always had a difficult time landing premium free agents, but Pollin signed Gilbert Arenas to a six-year, $65 million contract and gave Jerry Stackhouse a contract extension.

As a result, Pollin said he's had only a "few takers" on his refund offer, mostly from ticket brokers who made a living off Jordan's name and fans who had hoped for a Jordan-led playoff.

The franchise-record streak of 82 consecutive home sellouts Pollin enjoyed while Jordan was playing will almost certainly come to an end this season. In that context, Pollin made an extraordinary comment for a professional sports owner: He welcomes the fact that his team will have a lower profile this season.

"I'd like very much to have sort of a lower profile," he said. "We have a young team, and they have to mature, and I think the maturing process is going to take some time."

Pollin spoke excitedly about the new atmosphere and the changes made by Grunfeld and Eddie Jordan, but the owner realizes that it's the same unfulfilled excitement he's been showing for many unsuccessful years. The Wizards haven't been to the playoffs since 1997, haven't won a playoff game since 1988 and the franchise hasn't won a playoff series since 1982.

"It's been disappointing, but not frustrating," Pollin said. "I want to win. If I was in this business just for the money, I would be doing something else. But I love what I'm doing, and I love the team."

Pollin is one of the last of the old-school, family owners trying to stay competitive in an age when teams are owned by corporations and large partnerships. His shining moment came when his team won the NBA title in 1978, in an era before free agency, and the subsequent rampant increase in player salaries.

Even though he has a plan in place for a successor _ minority partner Ted Leonsis has first right to buy the team should Pollin decide to sell _ Pollin is determined to stick around until he wins that elusive second title.

"Yes, sir," Pollin said. "And then when I win the title, I'll consider what to do."

8

Businessman

Multimillion Dollar Gatorade
August 8, 1991
By Matt Kelley

Chicago Bulls' Michael Jordan drinks some Gatorade during a news conference in Chicago, August 8, 1991. (AP Photo/Mark Elias)

Chicago Bulls star Michael Jordan on Thursday formally announced he has signed a multimillion-dollar contract to endorse Gatorade, a sports drink that critics say may be no more effective than water.

Jordan, 28, the NBA's most valuable player in the 1991 championships, now endorses for 15 companies, including McDonald's hamburgers, Nike basketball shoes and Wheaties breakfast cereal. The Gatorade announcement came a week after a two-year agreement with Coca-Cola Co. expired.

"I think it's a relationship that through my profession is natural because of what I use Gatorade for," Jordan said at a news conference.

Gatorade is the best-selling brand for the Chicago-based Quaker Oats Co., said Quaker chairman William D. Smithburg. The exact terms of the Jordan contract were not announced, though published reports have put the deal at as much as $18 million over 10 years.

The announcement came a few days after an article in a consumer newsletter said sports drinks like Gatorade are no better than water for most amateur athletes.

Consumer Reports on Health, an advertising-free newsletter produced by the Consumers Union, reported in its August issue the results of a study it said criticized most sports drinks as frivolous.

The report cited a U.S. Army study that compared the performances of exercising men who used a Gatorade-like drink, sweetened water or plain water. The results showed that sports drinks aren't any better than water, said Dr. Murray Hamlet of the Army institute that performed the study.

"Gatorade is the greatest sales job since P.T. Barnum," Hamlet told the Chicago Tribune.

But Gatorade's president, Peter Vitulli, said Thursday that the Army study used a drink with less sodium and glucose than Gatorade. Vitulli said the drink, developed in 1965 by a University of Florida professor for the school's football team, has been studied at universities around the world and has proven its effectiveness.

"Of course it has different effects for different people," Vitulli said. "But we think it does what it does very well."

Be Like Mike, Part II
February 4, 1998
By Herbert G. McCann

Gatorade is betting you'll want to be like Mike all over again.

The catchy jingle that burst over the airways in 1991 accompanied by shots of Michael Jordan gulping down Gatorade helped cement Gatorade's hold on the sports-drink market.

Now, six years after dropping the tune that told weekend athletes they could "Be like Mike," Gatorade is bringing back what became an icon of pop-sports culture.

This time in addition to Jordan, the jingle will augment a Gatorade ad featuring, among others, Larry Bird, WNBA star Sheryl Swoopes, broadcaster and former wide receiver Ahmad Rashad and ESPN studio host Chris Berman.

Sports legends Michael Jordan and Mia Hamm take a moment in honor of their distinction as Gatorade's first male and female athletes during the brand's 50th anniversary celebration, in Paradise Valley, AZ., January 31, 2015. (Steve Boyle/Gatorade via AP Images)

The ad will first air during Saturday's NBA All-Star show and will run into early summer, when consumption of Gatorade is peaking.

"People have been asking about it since 1992," said Sue Wellington, vice president of marketing for Gatorade. "It really became a part of the pop culture."

Just as important for Gatorade, the popularity of the jingle allows its ads to break through the advertising clutter and stand out from the other products Jordan endorses, among them Nike Inc., Sara Lee Corp.'s Hanes underwear and Ball Park Franks, Wilson Sporting Goods and Bijan, maker of Michael Jordan Cologne.

James Bell, a partner in the New York product identity consulting firm of Lippincott & Marguilies Inc., says his firm usually counsels against using celebrities in favor of promoting the uniqueness of the product.

"I think the one danger I see in using people who are megastars is that he may outshine the product," Bell said. "You always need to keep your spokesman in line with the product you are trying to sell."

But although the jingle has been off the air since 1992, Bell said he remembers it having a nice warm tone that made Jordan out to be an approachable star, and made kids and adults want to be like him.

Gatorade, made by Chicago-based Quaker Oats Co., is the nation's leading sports drink, with U.S. sales of $1.3 billion last year. It has 80 percent of the sports drink market.

It is being challenged by Pepsi Cola's AllSport and Coca-Cola's Powerade, each with about 7 percent of the market, said Gary Hemphill, vice president of Beverage Marketing Corp., a research and consulting firm.

"Gatorade has lost some share, but they have managed to sustain strong growth," he said. "They have done a good job of promotion and distribution."

Hemphill said the old jingle helped make Gatorade the dominant sports drink.

"The goal of the others is to be a meaningful number two," he said.

The new ad, created by Chicago-based Foote, Cone and Belding, begins with a chiseled Jordan walking through a tunnel with the jingle playing in the background. In between shots of Jordan playing basketball, working out and drinking Gatorade are shots of Rashad, Berman, WNBA star Lisa Leslie and Swoopes singing. Others adding their vocals to the mix are the Grammy Award-winning group Take Six, John Popper of the band Blues Traveler and Los Angeles-based blues singer and actor Ernie Banks.

Not joining in the singing is Bird, dressed immaculately and seen sitting in an airplane. As the jingle's last words, 'Oh, if I could be like Mike,' fade out, the three-time NBA most valuable player and coach of the Indiana Pacers says, "I'm not going to sing."

Space Jam
November 26, 1996
By Bob Thomas

Chicago Bulls Michael Jordan poses with a cutout of Bugs Bunny at a news conference, in New York. Warner Bros. announced at the meeting the Jordan will join Bugs, and other members of the Looney Tunes family in an original live action/animation feature called "Space Jam" scheduled to begin production this summer for release in late 1996. The film will be directed by Ivan Reitman, June 20, 1995. (AP Photo/Marty Lederhandler)

Bugs Bunny never had it so good.

With more than a little help from his friend Michael Jordan, the debonair hare launched Warner Bros.' feature animation program with a smashing $48.5 million two-week take for "Space Jam."

The achievement marked the first time a rival has made a serious dent in Disney's virtual monopoly of the feature animation market. Don Bluth's "An American Tail," sponsored by Steven Spielberg, had a splurge in 1986 with a box-office gross of $47,483,002, but most other contenders have flopped.

Max Howard, president of Warner Bros. Feature Animation, admitted he didn't expect the impressive showing of "Space Jam":

"The cartoon characters hadn't been known for being in a feature. Michael Jordan had a following, but not as an actor. We were happily surprised that it has attracted a wide audience. The teen-agers are very solidly there. But we are attracting adults as well, especially those who are interested in the animation medium."

The British-born Howard, an animation veteran at 44, dodged the analogy of "Snow White and the Dwarfs," the 1937 film that launched feature animation for another company.

"We were lucky to be able to use all the classic characters of Warner Bros. cartoons," he pointed out, "whereas `Snow White' introduced a whole new group of characters. We were able to profit from all the great talents who made the public love the `Looney Tunes.' "

The usual question: What can Warners Feature Animation do for an encore?

"Our encore is `The Quest for Camelot,' " Howard replied. "We have a number of projects in various stages of development, so while we were working on `Space Jam,' we also were making `The Quest for Camelot,' which will come out at this time next year. That is a fully animated feature.

"We are working on different films, and I'm hoping we will develop more films that will combine live action with animation."

The longtime goal is to produce one feature a year, or at least every 18 months. Aside from choosing suitable subjects, a major concern is finding enough talent.

"As you must be aware, talent for animation films is at a premium today, because so many studios are making them," Howard commented. "The talent pool is very small, although there are a lot of artists coming into the business. The success of animated films is attracting a whole new group of artists who want to have careers in this medium."

He believes there is room in the marketplace for more animated features _ "as long as they are good."

Warner Bros. has been in the cartoon business since 1930, when the company released the first "Looney Tunes" (a play on Disney's Silly Symphonies). "Sinking in the Bathtub" starred Bosko, a cheerful creature in a derby hat.

Over the years the casts were augmented with Porky Pig, Bugs Bunny, Daffy Duck, Elmer Fudd, Tweedy Bird, Pepe LePew, Wile E. Coyote, Speedy Gonzalez, Foghorn Leghorn, Sylvester and Road Runner.

A crew of gifted animators created the Warner Bros. style: violent, irreverent, hilarious. The legendary Mel Blanc provided most of the starring voices.

Three years ago, said Howard, Warner Bros. recognized there was a market for well-made animation features.

"I think Warners realized that if you wanted to get into these films, you had to create the structure for them," he said. "That meant building a studio and permanently employing animators and artists."

The company now employs more than 550 at its suburban Glendale animation studio and one in London. And Howard continues to "scour the world" for additional talent.

Computer imagery played an important role in "Space Jam" and will continue to be used in future films. Computers also supply the colors. But Howard emphasized that animation is mostly done the old-fashioned way: by hand.

He wouldn't reveal the cost of "Space Jam," saying only that animation features are "very expensive, very labor intensive, and they take a long time to produce."

Once a child actor, Max Howard grew up in the English theater. He joined Disney in 1986 to run the London studio where "Who Framed Roger Rabbit" was produced. He supervised the financial, training and operations aspects of the Disney studios in Orlando and Paris and worked on various Disney features until moving to Warner Bros. 18 months ago.

CEO of Nike
January 19, 1999
By William McCall

The banner at Nike headquarters read: "Thanks Mike. Now don't be late for work." Retired NBA superstar Michael Jordan was officially welcomed to his other job as CEO by the company that has sold $2.6 billion in basketball shoes with his name.

Nike named Michael Jordan chief executive officer of its Brand Jordan division more than a year ago in preparation for the day when the Chicago Bulls guard would hang up his own basketball shoes for good. When that day arrived Wednesday, Nike chairman and founder Phil Knight, who hired Jordan to endorse the swoosh as an NBA rookie nearly 15 years ago, found a lump in his throat. "This really is it," Knight said. "This great artistry you're not going to be able to see any more." He denied reports that he visited Jordan last weekend in an attempt to talk him out of retiring. "First of all, I know it wouldn't do any good if I did try," Knight said.

The famous Nike Michael Jordan image graces the front of the Niketown store in downtown Portland, Ore., June 23, 2010. (AP Photo/Don Ryan, File)

"The day was coming. If it wasn't going to be this year it was going to be next year." The trick now is to bank on the charisma Jordan built up as perhaps the most recognizable athlete on the planet to push his line of shoes and clothing with his slam-dunking silhouette logo rather than the swoosh. Knight is certain the Jordan name will fly. "Absolutely," Knight said. "It's just gone beyond a level than anybody could have foreseen." It's a level of popularity Nike hopes to spread across all its products as the world's largest athletic shoe company emerges from a year of declining profits, layoffs and budget cuts set off by the Asian recession.

"Everything has gone horrible for them in the past year," said analyst Jennifer Black of Black & Co. in Portland. "There's been nothing but negative on the horizon for Nike for such a long time." Knight sees the retirement as the beginning of Jordan the legend, bigger than the game, even bigger than Babe Ruth or Muhammad Ali, who didn't have the worldwide reach provided by technology such as personal satellite dishes or 24-hour sports on cable TV. "I don't think you're going to see anything like this for quite a while," Knight said. "This is something very, very special." Overseas, Jordan has been compared to such American exports as Coca-Cola and Mickey Mouse, and is a huge star in places where basketball is barely even followed. "The notion is that Jordan is obviously one of the few athletes who transcends sport," said Josie Esquivel, an analyst with Morgan Stanley in New York. "He has this appeal that makes him a great ambassador for sports of any kind.

The corporate executives certainly believe that mantra, but I think you have a large number of people who believe that too." Knight said Jordan will be personally involved in product development as CEO for a line featuring a single style of shoe that sold $130 million in the first year alone.

"It was huge when it first arrived," said John Horan, publisher of Sporting Goods Intelligence, an athletic shoe industry newsletter in Glen Mills, Pa. "Nobody had seen anything like it. It was a big deal then, and it's a big deal now." Last year, sales reached $350 million, almost 4 percent of the $9.2 billion in revenue for Nike. "If you took the Jordan brand out of Nike, it would still be the No. 2 basketball company in the world next to Nike," said Vizhier Mooney, spokeswoman for Nike's basketball operations. But Horan said the timing actually may have been for the best, not only for Nike, Jordan and Knight, but for the NBA.

"The good part is that Air Jordan had gotten a little long in the tooth," he said. "Dynasties, after a while, can be boring. It was kind of time from the NBA standpoint for some new blood there."

9

Billionaire Owner

Owning a Team
June 15, 2006
By Jenna Fryer

Charlotte Bobcats new head coach Sam Vincent, right, holds a jersey with part-owner of the team Michael Jordan, left, during a news conference in Charlotte, N.C., May 25, 2007. (AP Photo/Chuck Burton)

Michael Jordan became part-owner of the Charlotte Bobcats on Thursday in a deal that gives him a stake in most of Robert Johnson's ventures.

Jordan's investment makes him second to only Johnson as the largest individual owner of the Bobcats. Johnson, who was awarded the expansion Bobcats three years ago, then named Jordan the managing member of basketball operations.

"I'm thrilled to have my friend, Michael Jordan, join me in my business and sports pursuits," Johnson said in a statement. "I not only respect Michael for his basketball knowledge and expertise, but also for his business skills, particularly in branding and marketing.

"Michael will provide invaluable management input to a Bobcats team that is poised to deliver results for the 2006-2007 season and beyond."

Charlotte Hornets
May 21, 2013
By Steve Reed

Charlotte Bobcats owner Michael Jordan speaks to fans before unveiling the new Charlotte Hornets logo during a ceremony at an NBA basketball game between the Charlotte Bobcats and the Utah Jazz in Charlotte, N.C., December 21, 2013. (AP Photo/Chuck Burton)

Michael Jordan wants to "bring the buzz back" to Charlotte.

The Bobcats owner said at a press conference Tuesday evening he's changing his team's name to the Charlotte Hornets beginning in 2014-15.

Jordan said he submitted an application to the NBA board of governors earlier Tuesday informing them of his decision and is optimistic the board will approve the name change when they convene in July.

"Let's bring the buzz back, and bring that energy back on the basketball court and make this city proud again," Jordan said.

Charlotte will remain the Bobcats next season, but if all goes as planned Jordan anticipates his team will become the Hornets the following season.

Jordan said his organization is giving the fans what they want.

"We spoke to our season ticket holders and fans, and overwhelmingly you guys wanted the Hornets name back," Jordan said. "And we went out and brought the name back."

NBA deputy commissioner and COO Adam Silver previously said it would take about 18 months for the Bobcats to change their name, but pointed out the fact that the league owns the rights to the name Hornets could help speed up the transition process.

Silver said in the April interview the name change would be "an enormously complex process and a very expensive process for the team. From everything to the uniforms, to the building, to the letterhead to the signs on the offices — "all of that has to be taken into account."

Pete Guelli, Charlotte's executive vice president and chief sales marketing officer, estimated the cost of changing the name to the Hornets at about $4 million. He added, however, that the decision wasn't based on money and that "nothing was going to keep us from going down this road because this is what the fans wanted."

Jordan knows that it will take more than just changing the name of the front of the jersey to turn his struggling franchise around — it will take talent. The Bobcats are 28-120 over the past two seasons, the worst record in the league.

"Ultimately we still have to play the game at a high level, which is what the Hornets did for a long period of time," Jordan said. "Changing the name does not guarantee that we're going to be a playoff-contending team. We still have a lot of work to do to build that. I'm not walking away from that. It is what it is."

He said it's too early in the process to know if the team will keep the Hornets' teal and purple colors.

The NBA's Hornets resided in Charlotte from 1988-2002 before then-owner George Shinn moved the team to New Orleans following a financial dispute with city officials over replacing the Charlotte Coliseum. Shinn wanted a new arena with additional luxury suites.

The New Orleans Hornets, now owned by Tom Benson, recently changed their name to the Pelicans.

Charlotte was awarded an expansion team in 2003 and then-owner Bob Johnson named the team the Bobcats. The venture was a financial disaster for Johnson, who lost millions before selling majority ownership to Jordan in 2010.

Even with Jordan at the helm, the Bobcats have never come close to matching the popularity of the Hornets, a team which sold out 364 straight home games, a streak that stretched nearly nine full seasons.

Since 2010 three Charlotte area residents have been leading a grass roots movement to persuade Jordan to bring back the popular Hornets nickname.

John Morgan, an elementary art teacher in Monroe, N.C., started a campaign on Facebook three years ago called "We Beelieve" after watching the Bobcats lose to the Orlando Magic in the franchise's only postseason appearance. Disappointed over the lack of energy in the arena, Morgan began longing for the days of Larry Johnson, Alonzo Mourning and Muggsy Bogues.

He wanted the Hornets name back and began gathering signatures to support his cause.

Shortly thereafter, brothers Scotty and Evan Kent took the effort a step further and created a website called "Bring Back the Buzz."

Eventually the three men pooled their resources for one common goal.

"It's amazing," Morgan said earlier Tuesday after reading reports of the pending name change. "It feels like I'm walking on a cloud."

While the Hornets name had no meaning for the city of New Orleans, it does have significance to native Charlotteans.

According to the Mecklenburg Historical Association, British general Lord Charles Cornwallis called Charlotte "a hornet's nest of rebellion" after city residents drove the British out of the area in 1780.

The tenacious moniker has become a source of pride for the city for more than two centuries. Charlotte Mecklenburg County police officers still wear a patch with a beehive stitched on their uniforms.

Front Office Success
October 28, 2014
By Steve Reed

Michael Jordan is learning how to win without scoring a basket. His Charlotte Hornets are winning and enter the season with high expectations. Jordan appears to be finally changing the losing culture around his franchise.

Looking relaxed, the six-time NBA champion smiled Tuesday as he talked about how gratifying winning a seventh would be — as if he knows something the rest of the NBA doesn't.

Jordan said helping the Hornets win their first NBA title as an owner is something that drives him in his post-playing career. The Hall of Famer said it would be more rewarding because it's tougher being an owner than it is being a player.

"I can impact the game in shorts and tennis shoes," Jordan said at a press conference at the team's downtown arena. "When I had those on it was easy to prove people wrong. It's hard to do that now when I have a suit on. I have to rely upon other people understanding my message and my focus."

But he can take some satisfaction knowing he has the Hornets heading in the right direction.

Charlotte is coming off a 43-39 season and Jordan hopes that with Lance Stephenson joining Al Jefferson and Kemba Walker, the building blocks are in place for his small-market team to make a run at the title.

Jordan took over as the Hornets primary owner in 2010 and made a commitment shortly thereafter to "strip things down." For him, that meant breaking up a playoff team he felt was decent, but not good enough to win a championship. So Charlotte jettisoned players like Gerald Wallace and Stephen Jackson and began the process of rebuilding.

It meant suffering through a 7-59 season, the worst in NBA franchise history.

"That is tough for a competitor like me," Jordan said. "But it left me even more determined to turn thing around."

Things seem to be headed in that direction — with Jordan often helplessly sitting courtside in a suit.

Mark Price, who played 12 seasons in the NBA, said he can relate to how hard it is for Jordan not to be able to throw on a No. 23 jersey and take the floor.

"Mike wouldn't have achieved what he achieved in his life if he hadn't been a super competitive person," said Price, now an assistant coach for the Hornets. "You don't lose that. So he's trying to have an impact as an owner."

Trying to find how to do that has led to criticism of Jordan — that his hands-on involvement has resulted in poor personnel decisions and losing records.

But the Hornets recent success and promising outlook is vindication for Jordan.

"We all want to be a part of something successful and to do that you have to make a mistake here or there," Jordan said. "There's not one successful person in his life that has not made mistakes. You try to learn from those mistakes and make sound decisions going forward."

Hornets coach Steve Clifford said Jordan is learning how to successfully compete from the front office.

The coach points to the free agent acquisitions of Jefferson — a third-team All-NBA selection last season — and Stephenson the last two years as examples of him upgrading the team's roster.

The coach said Jordan won't ever accept losing and that "he's done everything an owner can do to help his team."

"I know there is only so much he can do, and I know he'd like to suit up and come out and play with us — and we would like that, too," Jefferson said. "But he's having an impact in other ways."

Jordan invested $41 million over three seasons in Jefferson last year and $27 million over three years in Stephenson.

The Hornets also agreed to a four-year, $48 million contract extension Tuesday with point guard Kemba Walker, a person familiar with the deal said. The person spoke on condition of anonymity to The Associated Press because the deal had not been announced publicly.

"I don't think people have any idea of how involved he is in personnel decisions and the draft," Clifford said.

Clifford said the five-time NBA Most Valuable Player and 14-time All-Star gives "very constructive advice" to coaches and players when he sees things that might help the team or an individual improve — without crossing the line.

"He will make sure I know his opinion," Clifford said. "But the thing he always says is 'you're the coach. You do what you want, but this is what I see.'"

And what Jordan clearly envisions down the road is a championship.

Greatest Ever

A Little Anarchy
January 15, 1999
By Jim Litke

The best thing about retiring from the NBA when he did, Michael Jordan said, was taking the bragging rights with him. That, and leaving a few long-suffering friends behind.

"Patrick will never be able to live with himself because he can't beat Michael Jordan in a playoff series," he said. "And I told Charles he'd never win because he didn't dedicate himself."

That would be Patrick Ewing and Charles Barkley, but had Jordan gone down the list of people he called to gloat the night before his I'm-outta-here announcement, the retirement bash might be going on still.

With the exception of the 1994 and 1995 finals - Jordan was playing baseball the first year and scraping the rust off his game the second - the road to the NBA championship during the decade didn't so much go through Jordan and Chicago as dead-end there.

Ewing found himself staring at that brick wall more times than he cares to remember. Barkley played a brilliant Game 5 in the 1993 finals, bragged about saving the city from a championship-sized riot, then went back to Phoenix and got beat, anyway. The club they belonged to was hardly exclusive.

Karl Malone and John Stockton, Gary Payton and Shawn Kemp, Shaquille O'Neal and Penny Hardaway, Alonzo Mourning and Larry Johnson, Clyde Drexler - all were issued membership cards and badges. So were coaches Pat Riley, Lenny Wilkens, Larry Bird and Jeff Van Gundy, who looked beat-up even before Jordan laid a finger on him - all of them had cameos in those championship videos the NBA sells for $ 19.95 at season's end.

No doubt those tapes will be harder to peddle at the end of this one. Beyond Jordan's departure, there will be lingering resentment over the six-month lockout and the perception that 50 games is more a quiz than a full exam.

About the only thing the league has going for it at the moment is unpredictability. That will be the theme, if not the buzzword, in league slogans this year. (So much for "fan-tastic.")

All we know is who won't win: the Bulls. And the Clippers, not just because of their star-crossed past, but because of their star-crossed present. Shades of Danny Ferry: No. 1 draft choice Michael Olowokandi got tired of waiting for the lockout to end and signed with Kinder Bologna in the Italian League, where he is committed to play until Feb. 15.

After eliminating the Clippers, though, rule out anyone at your own risk. The new contract means less mobility for free-agents in coming years, and this season, it means the signing period will be measured in days rather than weeks. The balance of power could shift daily. With Jordan gone, anything will seem possible once more.

Deals will forge new allies; Latrell Sprewell could wind up working for Pat Riley. Other alliances will have to be shored up. Word is already circulating among the players that Detroit superstar Grant Hill and San Antonio's Tim Duncan are in for rough treatment because they weren't militant enough for some of their union brothers while the negotiations dragged out. On such things will the season turn.

Ultimately, a little anarchy will be a good thing. It will create new rivalries, new heroes and villains, shift the focus away from who left to those he left behind. The older Jordan got, the more the desperate the NBA became trying to line up his successor. Shaq, Penny, Hill, Allen Iverson, Kobe Bryant - all those players and more have auditioned for the part. But the lesson the league should have learned from Jordan is that stardom is grasped, not handed to somebody because they look good in a shoe commercial.

Jordan could do that, too. But it wasn't a means for him, or an end, just a way to pocket some extra money. He issued more challenges and talked more smack on the basketball court than he did in all those clever ads combined. And he came ready to back it up every night.

When that changed, when he had doubts, rather than coast through even one game, Jordan walked away.

"I had to be 'on' every game, not one-fourth of the time," he said. "I can't honestly say it will be there 82 times when I walk into the building. I've always been sure about that; now, I'm unsure about it."

Things could change over the next few weeks, but right now only one team looks ready to bring it every night. It's the same team that has been working out together most every day. Its attitude was adjusted by a coach who knows a little about competitive demands and it was beaten last season by the guy who practically wrote the book.

That's right. The championship road this year runs through Indiana.

Afterword

Decorated Career
By Jim Litke
January 14, 1999

- As a freshman at North Carolina, hits game-winning basket for Tar Heels in the NCAA championship game against Georgetown. 1982-1983

- AP All-America first team.

- Sporting News College Player of the Year.

- Sporting News All-America first team. 1983-1984

- AP All-America first team.

- AP College Player of the Year.

- Sporting News College Player of the Year.

- Sporting News All-America first team.

- After declaring himself eligible for the NBA draft following his junior year, is chosen third overall by the Chicago Bulls, behind Hakeem Olajuwon and Sam Bowie.

- Member of United States gold medal-winning Olympic basketball team. 1984-1985

- Named NBA Rookie of the Year after averaging 28.2 points. 1985-1986

- Missed 64 games due to a foot injury.

- Scores playoff-record 63 points in a first-round game against Boston. 1986-1987

- Sets NBA record by scoring 23 consecutive points against Atlanta.

- NBA Slam Dunk Champion.

- Scores 3,041 points, the third highest total in NBA history. Only Wilt Chamberlain reached that plateau.

- Averages 37.1 points to win first of seven straight NBA scoring titles.

- Only player in NBA history to record at least 200 steals (236) and at least 100 blocked shots (125) in the same season.

- Named All-NBA first team for first of seven straight seasons. 1987-1988

- NBA Slam Dunk Champion.

- Averages 35 points.

- NBA regular-season MVP.

- NBA Defensive Player of the Year.

- NBA All-Star Game MVP.

- Leads NBA in steals 3.2 per game.

- Named NBA All-Defensive first team for first of six straight years. 1988-1989

- Averages 32.5 points. 1989-1990

- Scores career-best 69 points against Cleveland on March 28.

- Leads NBA in steals 2.77 per game.

- Averages 33.6 points. 1990-1991

- Averages 31.5 points.

- NBA regular-season MVP.

- Named NBA Finals MVP.

- Leads Bulls to NBA championship.

- AP Male Athlete of the Year. 1991-1992

- Averages 30.1 points.

- NBA regular season MVP.

- Named NBA Finals MVP for the second straight year, the first player ever so honored.

- Scores playoff record 135 points (45 pg) in leading the Bulls to a three-game sweep of Miami in the first round. Included is a 56-point performance, his fifth career game of at least 50 points in the playoffs, an NBA record.

- Leads Bulls to NBA championship.

- Member of United States gold medal-winning Olympic basketball team.

- AP Male Athlete of the Year. 1992-1993

- Averages 32.6 points to tie Wilt Chamberlain's NBA record of seven straight scoring titles.

- Scores his 20,000th point, becoming the second fastest to reach that plateau.

- Posts highest scoring average in NBA Finals history, averaging 41.0 points against Phoenix as Bulls "three-peat" in six games.

- Leads Bulls to NBA championship.

- Named NBA Finals MVP for a record third straight season.

Chicago Bulls' Michael Jordan poses alongside his likeness on a box of Wheaties during an unveiling ceremony. Jordan is the seventh celebrity athlete to have his image displayed on a box of the cereal marketed as The Breakfast of Champions, October 31, 1988. (AP Photo/Mark Elias)

THE AP EMERGENCY RELIEF FUND

When Hurricane Katrina hit the Gulf Coast in 2005, many Associated Press staffers and their families were personally affected. AP employees rallied to help these colleagues by setting up the AP Emergency Relief Fund, which has since become a source of crucial assistance worldwide to AP staff and their families who have suffered damage or loss as a result of conflict or natural disasters.

Established as an independent 501(c)(3), the Fund provides a quick infusion of cash to help staff and their families rebuild homes, relocate and repair and replace damaged possessions.

The AP donates the net proceeds from AP Essentials, AP's company store, to the Fund.

How to Give

In order to be ready to help the moment emergencies strike, the Fund relies on the generous and ongoing support of the extended AP community. Donations can be made any time at http://www.ap.org/relieffund and are tax deductible.

On behalf of the AP staffers and families who receive aid in times of crisis, the AP Emergency Relief Fund Directors and Officers thank you.

AP

ALSO AVAILABLE FROM AP EDITIONS

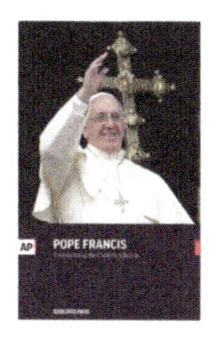

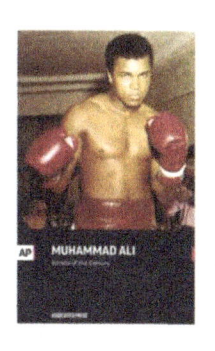

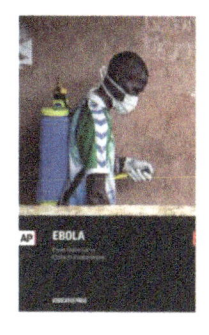

- THE FALL OF THE BERLIN WALL
- POPE FRANCIS
- CHRISTIANS UNDER ATTACK
- THE HUBBLE SPACE TELESCOPE
- THE COLLAPSE OF THE SOVIET UNION
- MUHAMMAD ALI
- MARIJUANA NATION
- EBOLA
- WARREN BUFFETT

CPSIA information can be obtained at www.ICGtesting.com
Printed in the USA
LVOW02s0040150915

454205LV00035B/385/P

9 781633 531499